MANAGING MAILER

Joe Flaherty

MANAGING MAILER

Coward-McCann, Inc. New York

Copyright © 1969 and 1970 by Joe Flaherty

All rights reserved. This book, or parts thereof, may not be reproduced in any form without permission in writing from the Publisher. Published on the same day in the Dominion of Canada by Longmans Canada Limited, Toronto.

Library of Congress Catalog Card Number: 71-104682

PRINTED IN THE UNITED STATES OF AMERICA

VAN REES PRESS • NEW YORK

FOR: The memory of my father, John, that for a while sustained me, and my mother, Maggie, whose toughness made me endure, and also Carolyn for the precious gifts of time, love, and memories

Acknowledgments

In any enterprise of pith and moment, one has many allies to praise. I was most fortunate in my endeavor. Jack Banning supplied me with invaluable tapes of the candidates' speeches, which Carolyn Mason generously transcribed. Alice Krakauer and Karen Berger kindly gave me access to their press files. And homage must be paid to the host of readers of this manuscript who pointed out many of the author's booberies. But special love must go to David and Elaine Markson for wading through the author's nightmare, his own galleys.

Through the stumbling odyssey of life, one is affected uniquely by rare accidents of persons and places, so for reasons of my own I would like to bow to Joe O'D, Richard Solomon Delaney, Connie Steinman, Ace Gillen—wherever they are—and the bygone balconies of the Paramount and the Roxy.

But like the child, one savors the best for last. And that icing is Jeanine. For it was her love and devotion and sound advice that helped bring this book to life. Not since Sam Spade was blessed with Effie has a man ever had such an extraordinary broad to help him through a caper.

JOE FLAHERTY

New York City
February 16, 1970

Contents

	ACKNOWLEDGMENTS	7
1.	IN THE BEGINNING...	13
2.	ON THE BANKS OF THE JORDAN	33
3.	TRYING TO MULTIPLY THE FISHES	69
4.	THE CONVERSION OF THE JEWS?	127
5.	THE SORROWFUL MYSTERIES ON THE WAY TO THE MOUNTAINTOP	165
6.	OUR NADA	197
7.	A SMALL BENEDICTION (EPILOGUE)	217

Illustrations following page 96

France was a land, England was a people, but America, having about it still that quality of the idea, was harder to utter—it was the graves at Shiloh and the tired, drawn, nervous faces of its great men, and the country boys dying in the Argonne for a phrase that was empty before their bodies withered. It was a willingness of the heart.

F. Scott Fitzgerald, *The Crack-Up*

"Ah, Frank," he said softly. "You've done grand things. Grand, grand things."
"Among others," Skeffington said.

Edwin O'Connor, *The Last Hurrah*

I
In the Beginning...

I T didn't begin as usual.

For more than a week in mid-March rumor had it that Norman Mailer was considering entry into the Democratic mayoral primary. From all reports the initial proposition for Mailer to enter the race had come from two disparate sources—Jack Newfield, the left-leaning political writer of the *Village Voice*, and Noel E. Parmentel, a conservative and contributor to William F. Buckley, Jr.'s right-wing organ, the *National Review*. This strange collision of minds was later to be characterized by Mailer as "the Hitler-Stalin pact."

On March 31 the summons came. Mailer's secretary, Carolyn Mason, called my desk at the *Village Voice* to inform me that Mailer was having a gathering at his Brooklyn Heights home to discuss the possibility of a mayoralty bid and I was invited to attend. Since I possess both a perverse sense of history and an ambitious journalistic mind, I accepted.

The meeting took place on the top floor of Mailer's brownstone, which directly overlooks the water and offers a panoramic view of New York—symbolically, I supposed, our military objective. The warmth of the room appealed to my Irish heart; it seemed like a blend of wood and whiskey, combining the best aspects of the womb and the coffin.

Books by the hundreds lined the walls, and to accentuate the sense of impending adventure, rope ladders hung from a planked ceiling, giving the room and its occupants a hint of voyage.

The assembled crew, though influential in their own circles, were hardly a gathering that would send chills up the wily spine of old John Bailey, the Democratic Party's majordomo. For the most part, it was literary.

New York magazine was represented by Peter Maas and Gloria Steinem. Maas—prematurely gray, a smoker of slim cigars, and a pursuer of elegance. But, somehow, the palette of his clothes seems to smudge—the Brooks Brothers jacket, conflicting with a little too much handkerchief, creates a style that might be described as Florentine Toots Shor. Steinem—a child from an industrial slum in Toledo, who found the glass slipper in New York and is now regarded as one of the city's Beautiful People, is blessed with a long mane of honey hair and elegant filly legs and a voice that doesn't want to go home again, so like Daisy's it reflects the sound of money.

From the *Voice*, besides Newfield, there was Mary Nichols, a handsome woman with a tough political mind and a nose for muckraking. And among the unattached political lights were novelist and former McCarthy speechwriter Jeremy Larner, a glacial young man with a reputedly dangerous temper hidden beneath the surface; Paul Gorman, also a McCarthy speechwriter—short, bearded, intense, who speaks with his hands and mouth simultaneously, not really speaking at all—more beseeching; and the journalist Pete Hamill, whose writing of late had taken the classical Irish journey back home to rediscover his roots and to find a mythical innocence he believes existed.

Then there was Mailer's regular entourage: former light heavyweight boxing champion José "Cheqüe" Torres, whose life-style has the ebullience of a bongo drum, though tonight he was saddened and muted by the fact that for ethnic reasons he had to remain loyal to Herman Badillo, the Puerto Rican mayoral candidate. And Buzz Farber, actor and Mailer's film partner, who gives you one of those muscular Robert Jordan handshakes that seems to signify the blowing of a bridge rather than a greeting.

And to flesh out the gathering there were the emissaries from different ideological camps. On the right were a criminal courts justice (who wished to remain anonymous) and Parmentel: the justice quiet and officious, Parmentel rangy and grim. One had noticed over the years two dominant traits in conservatives: their admirable penchant for tough, dull, infantry-type political work and their spectacular lack of humor. Later on I was to learn that Parmentel was disassociated from the former but had a franchise on the latter.

The eclipse of these gentlemen was Jerry Rubin—slight, shaggy, and gentle, sitting on a couch with his girlfriend, his makeup seemingly far removed from the exuberant name of the movement, Yippie, which he was supposed to or not supposed to lead.

Off on another plane was the Black lawyer and confidant of the Black Panthers, Flo Kennedy, possessing a face which has beauty because it is blatantly brazen. On the conventional side of reform politics was John Scanlon, a circular Irishman with a head of rusty curls. Scanlon, a friend and former Brooklyn coordinator for McCarthy and Paul O'Dwyer, was (for the lack of a more polite phrase) currently suffering from a case of political hot pants and was flirting with Brooklyn mayoral aspirant Hugh Carey, a hawkish Congressman whom he had opposed violently in the past.

Sitting on a stool in the rear of the room was Jimmy Breslin, the columnist and resident New York City "police station genius," as Philip Roth called him. Breslin's presence was significant, because a segment of the group felt he should be added to the Mailer ticket as candidate for president of the City Council to give the ticket, in Steinem's words, some "street smarts." But besides such a tactical reason, the political marriage of a Jew and an Irishman in this city always has been an asset, and my eyes began to frisk the room for an Italian controller.

For the first two hours serious politics was ignored and serious drinking explored. Mailer moved about the room, a tall iced bourbon in hand, chatting with individuals. At one point, he misplaced his original drink, made a fresh one, rediscovered his original, and then stood talking with a glass in each hand, adding new dimension to the term "a two-fisted politician."

Breslin, giving the lie to his prodigious myth, remained seated, drinking coffee and nervously chain-smoking cigars to offset the chain-smoking of cigarettes that he thought was killing him.

When the conversation turned to politics, it was mostly cute, smartass one-liners that hovered between limp wit and camp. Ice cubes and glasses continued to chime with churchly regularity, and the meeting was going nowhere. Newfield approached me to call the gathering to order, a request I found strange but nevertheless obeyed. Mailer stood before a circular table that was situated in front of the bay window, his bourbon like an ever present hand puppet accompanying him and the lighted skyline of the city serving as a backdrop. Only De Gaulle could have staged it better.

With his candidacy not yet conceived, still a gleam in his eye, Mailer proceeded to make his first political mistake. He asked a gathering of polemicists what they thought of his impending candidacy. The dialogue that followed could be matched only by the construction crew who worked on the Tower of Babel.

Parmentel immediately urged Mailer to run without Breslin. Farber, now slightly whiskied and feeling his loyalty usurped, urged the same with a dash of waspish venom. Newfield and Gorman thought Breslin was essential. Steinem reminded Mailer that women's liberation was a big issue. And Gorman noted that the high school kids were the most politically hip segment of the city's populace.

Hamill discouraged Mailer's candidacy by citing an evening that Mailer had coordinated in his home with politically influential people to support Herman Badillo, feeling any Mailer candidacy would be a betrayal of Badillo. Scanlon, the realist, politely found the whole thing absurd.

Flo Kennedy seized the floor and demanded that the yet unreleased sperm of Mailer's candidacy now travel a perverse route to give rebirth to Adam Clayton Powell for mayor with Mailer as his running mate. To which Breslin muttered, "We're fuckin' nuts, but he isn't even reliable." Rubin, not to be trumped by a conventional Negro on the ticket, quietly played his ace of spades: "Why not run a Black Panther?" By this time, I was contemplating the spiritual qualities of Carmine DeSapio and Richard Daley.

The burp-gun dialogue continued, and in despair I suggested we retire to the bar and get drunk. Mailer then made a valiant attempt to pull the evening together. Gently now he explained that he indeed was serious. "Camp and college-boy pranks are repulsive to me," he said, especially in a time when the city and many of its people were in such desperate shape. For the first time in the evening the chorus died, and a solo performance was taking place. It was to be short-lived.

When Mailer offered the main plank in his platform, "a hip coalition of the left and right," all hell broke loose again. The question of what the hell he meant reverberated around the room like a fancy billiard shot.

Larner vehemently declared that he didn't want anything to do with the right in this city and then turned to Gorman and said: "The major issue in this city is the white working class." He proceeded to leave, rendering Mailer his first political credentials—he lost cabinet members even quicker than Lindsay.

In the past Mailer had qualified his respect for the right. He wasn't talking about William Buckley, but more about guys he knew in the Army and those cats who rode motorcycles, and then with a smile: "But, of course, they put shit in the air with their exhaust fumes, too." Finding his theme, he began to expand in a style that was to remain constant throughout the campaign: crouched, the left hand pawing and developing into an effective jab when the tempo of his speech picked up, shifting weight from foot to foot in a wobble like an undecided tenpin.

"The hope is," he went on, "that a few sparks from the fires on the right and left will fly up and form this coalition." Flo Kennedy, representing her minority of one, took to the attack. She wanted to know *who* Mailer meant by the *left*. "Jack Newfield may be left to you, baby," she purred, "but he ain't to me."

Mailer admonished Kennedy for her attack on Newfield, to which she countered: "Norman, you don't know a goddamn thing about the Blacks."

Mailer, opting for the Brotherhood Award, replied with a satanic grin: "Flo, darling, to know one is to fuck one." The ice cubes in the glasses began to sound like nervous sleigh bells.

During all this, Rubin and Breslin had remained silent. Mailer then decided to seek their counsel: "Jerry, what do you think?"

Rubin couldn't understand why Mailer wouldn't run as an independent. "I don't care about these people [Democrats]. Why have anything to do with them?"

Mailer queried in the tones of a father confessor: "Jerry, do you believe in electoral politics?"

Rubin, delivering the doctrine of the dropout, gently replied, "No, Norman, electoral politics is not relevant."

"What do you believe in, Jerry—spirituality?"

"Yes. Spirituality, Norman."

"Then what about the spirituality of the machine? To make it hum, hum, hum..."

IN THE BEGINNING...

Suddenly, Rubin looked like a convert as the "hums" graced the air like so many Kyrie Eleisons.

Breslin apparently had had enough of the spirituality, the bickering, and the skirting of what he thought were the real issues. He exploded into a monologue that ran second only to Molly Bloom's. "Norman, stop the fuckin' Micky Mouse shit. There's no issues in this town. Leave that Micky Mouse shit to those other clowns. Just get on TV and look at the camera and say, 'All these other guys are full of shit.' So what if they blip you out. People will be able to read your lips. Every asshole sitting on a barstool in Brooklyn and Queens will fall on the floor laughing and run out and vote for you. Fuck issues—this city is lost.

"Everybody knows these other guys are crooks."

And to prove his point, he delivered a verbal dossier of Mafioso restaurants that would have made Craig Claiborne envious. What candidate from Brooklyn had shrimp scampi with a hood in Queens? And what guy from the Bronx was known to twirl his linguine with a Cosa Nostra family head in Red Hook?

We all sat like rapt students in awe at this seminar on gutters as Breslin reached his conclusion: "And, furthermore, I wouldn't even let Norman get on TV and debate these fuckin' bandits. He'd get arrested for consorting."

It became clear that nothing concrete was going to be decided. What we did settle on was that if there was going to be a ticket, it would be a Mailer-Breslin ticket. And the question of a candidate for controller was shelved for the future, although there was some support for Flo Kennedy (a Black on the ticket) and Gloria Steinem to attract the ladies. Kennedy flatly refused without a reason, and Steinem begged off by saying that her presence would damage the credibility of the ticket by making it look like "a campy literary exercise."

If we decided to run a controller, Mailer insisted it must be someone "hip." He went on to say that if we didn't have a hip candidate the newspapers would exploit the ticket. To prove his point, he cited an article in that day's New York *Times* for which a reporter had interviewed a collection of Jewish mothers who had prominent sons and daughters, the peg being—was Alexander Portnoy's complaint about his mother for real?

"Do you know what that goddamn New York *Times* did?" Mailer roared. "They got my mother to say that she was permissive with me when I was a child. Permissive! My mother has never used that fuckin' word before in her whole life!"

Also, if the campaign was going to take shape, Newfield suggested that John Scanlon and I manage it, since we had had organizational experience in the Lindsay, McCarthy, and O'Dwyer races in Brooklyn. Scanlon, now a deputy commissioner under Lindsay, refused. If he was to desert Lindsay, it would be to follow the star of fellow Democrat Hugh Carey.

I had my own doubts. First, I had a warm feeling for John Lindsay, who I thought was a courageous mayor trapped in a historical revolution; and his handling of that revolution is what moved me toward him. Black revolution in this country has been handled in three ways: repressing it, Wallace style; ignoring it, Nixon style; or encouraging it, Lindsay style.

Second, I wondered about my intentions. Like the rest of my breed who record everything from their first piece of ass to their last breath of air, I immediately sensed the possibilities of recording such a campaign. And there was also Mailer, whom I knew only on a casual but warm basis.

Would I be swallowed up with close association like so many others, or would I have to oppose him at every turn, regardless of substance, hysterically trying to maintain my own identity? Moreover, there was a personal reason. That once pleasant pastime, my drinking, had taken a dark turn and I had decided on a sabbatical. And even though I had managed to get through this evening on soda, I didn't need the warnings of a parish priest to tell me that Norman Mailer and James Breslin would provide spectacular occasions of sin.

Breslin, Hamill, Scanlon, and I left together. At the door Mailer was apologetic: "Look, I didn't mean the evening to go like this, all this boozing and partying. Why don't a small group of us get together tomorrow night to talk it over seriously. What the hell, at least everybody got everything off their chests tonight." We all were moved by his earnestness and agreed to another meeting at his home the next evening.

We had parted company with Breslin at the Hotel St. George and started down the street in search of a cab when we heard a rattle of dark laughter. We turned. Breslin stood on the sidewalk, his hands cupped around his mouth, shouting to the Brooklyn night: "Do you know something—that fuckin' bum is serious!"

The next evening Newfield, Gorman, Hamill, Torres, Breslin, and his wife, the former Rosemary Dattolico (whom Breslin describes as "very Italian and a lover of knives on black nights"), and I gathered at Mailer's. Breslin and Rosemary, after years of marriage, have developed several striking similarities. They both possess an easy, swaggering street charm, and their voices, like raspy matched turtle doves, have the same sandpaper eloquence. Her face is a chronicle of Breslin's past mischief, but tonight there seemed to be a line of censure etched in her smile which said: *I went along with you before, but enough is enough, you bastard.*

Drinks were consumed at a civil pace, and the conversation centered on what problems we might have to deal with if we decided to make the race. The first ticklish question we fielded was: Was Mailer eligible to run for office, since years before he had stabbed his third wife, Adele, and even though he'd received a suspended sentence he was in the eyes of the law a convicted felon? We decided we'd best check into the election law before we made any formal statement of candidacy to the press.

Breslin salvaged this embarrassing interlude by once again launching into the morality of the other candidates. "I swear to Christ, Norman, I'm going to get on TV and just yell 'Mafia.'" Then, turning to the assemblage, he asked: "How many of you clowns got records?"

The group, recalling everything from peace and civil rights busts to raps for drunken driving and barroom brawling, raised their hands in unison like a class of schoolboys at the question: Who wants permission to leave the room? Breslin just shook his head in despair, muttering, "What a fuckin' crew!"

After drinks we went to Foffé's restaurant, a favorite of Mailer's, in Brooklyn Heights and were joined by Scanlon and Joe Ferris. Ferris, a friend and neighbor from the Park Slope section of Brooklyn, is one of those Irish sons to whom mothers in their declining years, as their vision turns toward heaven, frequently refer as "a blessing." The largest part of his life is dedicated to myriad services for the people of the city outside any official capacity. He works with Black children in Bedford Stuyvesant and prisoners on Riker's Island and has helped form block associations in far-flung neighborhoods throughout Brooklyn. As a strong advocate of neighborhood control, he deals with government on its most local level, the city block. The more local the cause, the harder he works. The death of any brownstone, tree, or shrub in the city diminishes him. He has pursued all these causes in his basic blue suit, a garment one feels he first donned at his confirmation, that realized the spirituality of its owner and decided not to wear out but to grow with him. After Ferris had engaged Mailer in conversation for fifteen minutes, Mailer turned to me and remarked, "My God, he's a passion play."

The general feeling at the table was that if an assault was to be made upon the Democratic Party, this was an ideal year to try it because of the certified mediocrity of the field. Strangely enough for a party that is nationally talented, the Democrats in the foremost city in America (with the exception of the late Robert Kennedy, who was an import) are for the most part a measure below the bottom of the barrel. And this year the good bosses seemed to be digging deeper than ever to produce unearthly candidates.

First and foremost was the current controller, Mario Procaccino, who like an Italian Helen Morgan announced his candidacy amid a shower of tears because he "loved his city" so much. And to make his announcement even more ludicrous, as he stood there sobbing, TV reporter Gabe Pressman asked him in somber tones if he was "serious about his candidacy." Breslin's unsolicited advice was "if they want him to win, they'd better lock him up in a fuckin' broom closet."

Of the others who'd announced, we felt competition would come from Congressman Hugh Carey, a domestic liberal and Vietnam hawk who would invoke his connection with the Kennedy family to gain support. Then there was the liberal Bronx Congressman James Scheuer, who had been running an exorbitant campaign operation for months without creating any recognizable enthusiasm.

But the best of the lot was Bronx Borough President Herman Badillo, a former relocation commissioner in the Wagner Administration. Badillo was both intelligent and ambitious, but his vision did not seem to go beyond the old liberal canons of more public housing and bureaucratic poverty programs. His biggest problem was his personality. He possessed none of his Latin brothers' fire and life, and, indeed, in his dark Petrocelli suits he looked wooden—a Puerto Rican Robert Goulet.

But all voices concurred that the probable heavyweight of the field, now in distant Spain being beckoned home by some of the most powerful Democratic organizational voices in the city, would be that municipal Lazarus, the Honorable Robert F. Wagner, Jr.

Mailer was receptive to Ferris' ideas on "local democracy" and immediately applied them to his left-right coalition. He began to talk of neighborhoods forming so one might find his "own true life style." He raged against the liberal center that tried to force an across-the-board ideology for the whole city. Indeed, why not a day in Harlem to honor Malcolm X and a day in Staten Island to honor John Birch? How are any of us to know whose ideas are valid or not if we don't have a chance to express them? he asked. The basic point he stressed was that none of us knew who was right anymore.

I was intrigued. This expansion of fledgling ideas thrown out to him was something that would recur throughout the campaign, but it never ceased to amaze me. Presented a nugget of an idea that attracted him, Mailer would endlessly mine it into a mother-lode philosophy.

You realized that even when it was your own pet project your mind never carried it to the dazzling conclusion Mailer would offer days after hearing it. The idea of such a mind waging war on the Democratic Party was becoming an irresistible notion.

Moreover, an attack on institutionalized liberalism by a man of the left appealed to me. After years of playing the liberal game, one had begun to sour on his own participation. One recalled his vigorous defenses of public housing whose architectural style Mailer now dismissed as "Mussolini modern" and his participation in a city poverty program that was a sugar tit for the Blacks and a swindle to the whites.

But such thoughts were classified in liberal circles as the thoughts of a bigot. For one had come to believe that to the liberal mind Blacks and Puerto Ricans were adorable Hummel figures, objects for matronly maintenance, and that the working-class whites were singularly molded into an apotheosis—a burly, racist truck driver in a T-shirt with a cigar butt clenched in his teeth.

And like Mailer, as he wrote in *Miami and the Siege of Chicago*, I too had begun to tire of the tyranny of Black "soul." For I felt that they had no exclusivity on disgust with their country. Granted, it was doubtful that mine would ever lead to a rooftop with a gun, but it was present in a different form in me and many of my contemporaries. The tyranny I felt was similar to that of being the ward of a stingy aunt who knows well she has the money to illuminate the dark corners of the house but, perversely, with spite goes about unscrewing light bulbs, hoarding her treasure for the grave.

And liberalism would never be enough for the Blacks. They could legitimately claim it had not contributed enough; but diabolically it provided the self-defeating cushion on which to fall back—the Man. So it was for ambivalent reasons I wanted the Blacks to have full control of all measures of their lives: one, to end their insanity of not knowing whether they are a glorious race or mediocre like the rest of us; and two, to liberate myself from being viewed collectively, a role I didn't relish, since I liked to think that thirty-three years ago something unique had happened when I was conceived by an Irish dockworker and a domestic. And, too, many years ago I lost my taste for mouthing *mea culpas.*

Once again no definite decision to run or not was reached. Mailer was to leave for his summer home in Provincetown for two weeks to rest and think it over. We agreed he would remain in contact. Ferris stressed that a decision had to be made soon if we were to start circulating petitions to place Mailer and Breslin on the primary ballot. We had six weeks to obtain the necessary 5,000 signatures of registered Democrats, but since petitioning is a complex legal process (names can be negated for any number of picayune reasons), we felt that 15,000 signatures were needed to provide some insurance.

Our plight didn't seem to impress Mailer. With all the humility of De Gaulle he said, "Shit, if we can't get seventy-five thousand signatures in a couple of weeks, we have nothing going for us." I was speechless. Scanlon nearly choked. Ferris, like Mona Lisa, smiled his enigmatic smile. And Breslin, not to be outdone, shrugged with a nonchalance that suggested Mailer was being too modest.

During Mailer's absence, in an attempt to find out whether our trial balloon was full of hot air or not, we ran a full-page ad in the *Village Voice* asking for donations and volunteers. Within five days we received about 200 phone calls from people expressing their desire to work for a Mailer-Breslin ticket. By all political yardsticks this was a healthy response to a bastard candidacy, but Mailer, who was keeping in touch by phone, wasn't overly impressed. I began to get the feeling that he possessed a very conventional political trait—he wanted to be drafted by acclamation, or as Richard Nixon was fond of saying, he would "serve if destiny called."

On Sunday evening, April 6, Steinem held a meeting at her apartment in the East Seventies. The decor of her study, where we gathered, is a mass of ideological contradictions. It is wallpapered in a black and white zebra pattern similar to the motif of that bastion of decadent capitalism, the El Morocco, interrupted by posters of Che Guevara and Cesar Chavez, the leader of the California migrant grape pickers. Above a photograph of Robert Kennedy with his unruly hair is hung a collection of matched earrings in precise flight formation. The earrings were to provide the last semblance of order I was to witness that night.

The meeting then moved into her living room—large, attractive, painted a warm yellow, and furnished with those spartan chairs that are rewards for the adherents of Rye Crisp and Metrecal. A collection of new faces added spice to the gathering. They seemed to fall into natural groups, perhaps for ideological reasons or possibly because of the length of their hair. The shoulder-length group was made up of Richard Goldstein, pop critic; Bob Christgau, who writes a column on rock 'n' roll for the *Village Voice;* and Jeff Shero, editor of the underground paper *Rat.* Close-cropped were Geoff Stokes and Peter Linzer, both products of Manhattan's reform Democratic clubs and possessors of droopy walrus mustaches, and a young lawyer, Leon Friedman, author of a book titled *Southern Justice,* all present to advise us on the proper way to petition.

Doing solos were Ellen Willis, activist in Women's Liberation; Willie Smith, a minister and the former head of the city's Neighborhood Youth Corps, there at my request as a possible controller candidate; and Alice Krakauer, a former McCarthy press aide whose speech was riddled with psychological jargon but whose remedies were pure chicken soup, wearing a hat similar to the one Margaret Hamilton wore when she was the terror of the Münchens.

Maas took the floor and explained to the group what had taken place at previous meetings. After being subjected to the supreme torture of allowing someone else to speak for five uninterrupted minutes, the gathering let loose a salvo of questions when Maas came to the end of his summation. Christgau wanted to know if the positions on the ticket were firm—Mailer for Mayor, Breslin for president of the City Council. When he was told yes, he announced he was leaving because Mailer couldn't talk to the white working class in this city and "that's where the problem is at." Shero then joined his cause, and there was a full-scale rebellion taking place.

The Breslin proponents argued that Mailer—a Jewish novelist as impressive as any there was in Manhattan—didn't cut ice with the beer drinkers in Brooklyn and Queens. And following the line of Rap Brown, that the white man should civilize his own, they felt Jimmy was the man for the job. A show of hands was proposed to determine who should run on the mayoral line, and the room was equally divided: nine for Mailer, nine for Breslin.

I spoke next and tried patiently to explain that, though I appreciated the sentiment, you just can't shuffle National Book Award winners around like subservient aldermen, and the composition of the ticket already had been decided.

Maas and Steinem concurred, and I was spared my imagined horror of a midnight phone call to Provincetown to say, "Norman, you been dumped." Breslin, passing the evening at Shor's, never realized his brief flirtation with destiny.

The meeting proceeded to pass from crisis to chaos. Who should run as controller? Ellen Willis felt it had to be a woman; Shero wanted someone who could relate to the militant high school kids; others proposed a member of the Black Panthers. Stokes in despair offered: "All we need to find is a Black girl who carries a gun, goes to high school, and believes in abortion."

Goldstein, professing to have "a different head" from anybody in the room, found the whole thing irrelevant. "My wife and I were talking this morning," he said, "and we realized New York just isn't where it's at anymore, so we decided to buy land up in Woodstock." Josh Greenfeld, a writer who was covering the meeting for an upcoming book on the mayoral primary, added: "Yeah, Richie, but it would be a nice place to keep for a visit."

Willie Smith had been taking all this in, along with a good deal of scotch. Smith, a short Black man with a beard and Cagneyesque gestures, thought he smelled an easy honky kill in the confusion. "Look," he said, his hands forming into a stick-'em-up style, "I'm running for controller, and I'll tell you why." He launched into a five-minute tirade on why he should be our man. In a rhetorical style that is common among many Black leaders, he mixed gutter hip with Baptist revivalism. He stressed the allegiance he had with the tough Black kids of Brooklyn's Bedford Stuyvesant (a valid claim) and called himself "a true spokesman for the Black community, unlike the Panthers." But he made the mistake of underestimating his audience.

In a loud voice Shero said that Smith was "so much bullshit, since Panthers were being jailed while his ass was on a city payroll." Ellen Willis joined Shero on the attack, and Smith countered: "Look, I don't give a goddamn about your ladies' organization." The lady, much to Smith's chagrin, forgot her historical "place" and bristled: "You son of a bitch, don't call me nigger."

So the finale was that Smith had to settle for a snootful of free scotch; Breslin, though well loved, a second spot; and Mailer —in his bed in Provincetown—an uneasy crown.

That week on an evening news broadcast, Gabe Pressman broke an exclusive: Robert Wagner was entering the mayoral race. I called Mailer to tell him the news and to advise him to come back and declare. Wagner's entry put an antipolitical feeling in the city's air. A city in crisis looking for new leadership now was being offered a man who had been mayor for twelve spiritless years and then fled to Spain as ambassador when his administration's ineptitude began to catch up with him. New Yorkers, like all civilized people, find it difficult to revive passion for dead love affairs, and there was a jaunty feeling of "fuck-youism" running throughout the town, a feeling that was essential to a Mailer-Breslin ticket.

Though Mailer agreed with my prognosis, he refused to openly declare. We would work covertly, gathering petitions, and if things went well we would formally announce later. I felt he was hedging his ego against possible lack of interest in his candidacy.

He arrived back in town Sunday, April 13, for an 11 A.M. meeting at Steinem's. I arrived at 11:30 to find him sitting on the couch looking rested and slimmer. Without so much as a greeting, he snapped: "You're a half hour late. Let's make it on time in the future."

It was obvious Mailer was ready to meet the electorate. God only knew if the reverse held true.

2

On the Banks of the Jordan

O N Tuesday, April 15, Mailer decided to dip his toe into the political waters. Alice Krakauer, working out of her apartment, started to prepare a schedule of college speaking engagements at which Mailer and Breslin would attempt to raise troops.

The first of these was at Columbia University, where Mailer was to join a group of other speakers in denouncing the ABM. It wasn't the kind of kickoff Mailer relished. He felt the ABM was too easy a target. "The problem with liberals," he said, "is that they like to beat a dead horse. Who isn't against the ABM?"

I maneuvered with the coordinators of the Columbia rally to have Mailer speak last—a condition he demanded, since he didn't want his words to be sandwiched in between "so much dull liberal bullshit."

The meeting was held in Wollman Auditorium, a room—with its imitation wood paneling and deep blue fiber glass drapes—which is similar to and as sad as those suburban houses to which newlyweds flock in quest of gentried "class." Mailer, the champion of the baroque, was distressed. "This place is cancer," he said and observing the rather sedate audience added: "This isn't my kind of crowd."

Many of the students had seen the initial campaign ads in the *Voice* and approached him, offering encouragement. A young man, a love child with long hair and beads, told Mailer he would like to kiss him on the cheek for luck. The novice politician adroitly handled his first dilemma. "God," he said, "you'll ruin my campaign before it gets off the ground." And amid laughter he moved off, his record and his cheek unblemished.

Mailer sat in the front row while first a scientist and then a professor delivered a litany on the evils of the ABM. He seemed rather somnolent, as though he were listening to an old song, its reverie recalling no particular passion. Occasionally, he would shift in his seat, some irreverent perversity of the mind poking him.

Herman Badillo and his aides entered the hall and moved toward the stage. This was the first meeting between Badillo and Mailer since the evening at Mailer's home when Badillo left with the impression that he had Mailer's support, only to find out two weeks later that his benefactor was his Brutus.

Badillo, dressed in dark blue and looking eternally starched, took the stage and made short shrift of the ABM. Then he launched into a staccato chronicle of the need for a shift in our national priorities toward welfare and drug programs, creation of more jobs and housing, and combating crime, all urban-oriented and very much to do with becoming the mayor of New York City.

It was as impressive as any verbal political wind sprint I had ever heard. One young man, recovering from the blitz, muttered: "Yeah, but what about the fuckin' ABM?"

Now only Mailer was left. The students turned attentive with anticipation as he swaggered onto the stage, a finger of his left hand scratching his ear—he was a satanic Will Rogers. "I wasn't going to attend this meeting," he began, "because I figured it was just another liberal circle jerk." The kids roared their approval. And then, after a Jack Benny pause: "But when I started to run for mayor . . ." The laughter rose again, and he had them.

"I was sitting there," he went on, "trying to figure out a reason to defend the ABM, and I think I've found it." He proceeded to explain with convoluted brilliance how the ABM would keep the military sane, since they have a residual desire to carry on "local wars." He continued that with the ABM we would be able to launch a small rocket into North Vietnam; in turn the Chinese could send two back and knock out our site at Malmstrom; and everyone would be happy, save face, and the cities also would be saved. The previous speakers nervously sat fumbling sheets of statistics as Dr. Strangelove smiled at them in triumphant glee.

Mailer went into a rambling montage, inserting random thoughts as they occurred to him: the countryside was right—the cities were trying to overrun them; he preferred Nixon to Humphrey because Nixon was "a pure computer" and Hubert "a hysterical computer," and he'd take a pure computer anytime.

And summing up his philosophy, he said he was running on a left-right axis from "free Huey Newton to end fluoridation."

The network television reporters were stationed outside in the hall to interview the speakers, and Mailer got all the play. Badillo, looking grim, stood neglected on the sidelines. It was evident he realized that even if Mailer was not a threat numerically at the polls, he was going to be significantly damaging in two ways: the allegiance he commanded from the kids and the free television spots on the evening news he, with his freewheeling character, would steal from the other candidates—the spots Badillo so desperately needed in his low-financed campaign.

Badillo, accompanied by Torres, invited us to lunch at a Spanish restaurant, La Paella, a generous offer, I thought, in light of current events; but I was soon to realize that there is more than one way to pick up a check. At first, the conversation was general: boxing, writing, and political small talk. Mailer spoke about how quickly he could judge a good writer, just as Torres could assess a good boxer. The name of a married Badillo aide, who had recently made the wrong kind of headlines by getting caught with another woman, came up. The aide in question happened to be Jewish, and Badillo turned to Mailer and said, "You Jews ought to leave the women to the Latins. Jews just don't know how to handle them; it always ends up in trouble." Mailer gently countered: "I wish the hell you'd told me that years ago; you could have saved me four wives."

But it wasn't advice to the lovelorn Badillo really was interested in offering. To be sure, seduction was on his mind, but not of the traditional off-to-the-motel variety. The good screwing in question was Norman Mailer's mayoral candidacy. "You know, Norman," he said, "you'll never find out if you have any *real* support just by appearing on TV and speaking at colleges. You should do what I do. For the rest of the week, get up early and stand outside the subway stops in Brooklyn and the Bronx. Greet the people, and ask them if you should run."

Badillo's strategy was patently evident. The only exposure of Mailer's candidacy had appeared in the rather esoteric *Village Voice*, and though he was well known in the inner sanctums of Manhattan, his name—like the early Agnew—just wasn't a household word in the hinterlands of Brooklyn and the Bronx. Of course, Badillo envisioned Mailer, his unruly hair a mushroom cloud of curls, standing outside some subway stop on the Grand Concourse at an ungodly early hour and clutching an unsuspecting grandmother by the hand, saying: "I'm Norman Mailer, I want to be mayor," while she sprinted down the street shrieking: "Norman who?" Later on, Mailer and I agreed that if this was Badillo's idea of subtle seduction, then contrary to cliché, Latins must be lousy lovers.

The following Sunday Mailer was scheduled to appear at a Democratic reform club in Manhattan. We drove over in a rented limousine from Brooklyn with his daughters from his marriage to Adele, Betsy and Dandi. Betsy is a cute, shy ten-year-old who writes short stories, a fact that gives her father particular delight. Dandi is twelve years old, poised beyond her years, with skin the color of cocoa powder—a potential Gauguin beauty. Mailer, in a warm, relaxed mood, told us how, on reading *Studs Lonigan* as a boy, he wanted to become a writer.

The car dropped Mailer and me at 15th Street and went on to deliver the girls to their mother's home. Mailer wanted a drink before his speech, so, after rejecting one bar because "a drunken fag who was in one of my movies" was inside, we wound up getting his drink in a Chinese restaurant. This physical proximity of reform clubs and Chinese restaurants was to be one of the many observations James Breslin would make during the campaign.

The Tilden Democratic Club is located on Irving Place in the Gramercy Park area. It is housed on the ground floor of a town house which reflects memories of a more opulent era: fireplaces, decorative moldings, large mirrors topped with gilt eagles. And the audience, too, was part of another time—not the fleshy era of the house, but a time when "civility" was abroad in the city, when the Blacks were not Blacks but Negroes, when poverty programs were regarded by their recipients as benevolent blessings, and when the Jews were viewed by the Blacks as descendants of Eleanor Roosevelt, enlightened allies, not "kike" shopkeepers and deadeners of Black minds in classrooms.

Mailer's presence was an intrusion; no, more a raid, for what he brought with him was the truth of the time, the disease of the sixties.

He had a new touchstone for his platform. His candidacy would embody New York City's becoming the fifty-first state of the union. It was an idea he had acquired from Clay Felker, editor of *New York* magazine, who (I presumed) got it from Pete Hamill, who had written about the notion on several occasions, who may have lifted it from the late William Randolph

Hearst, since it was one of his pet editorial projects, who in all likelihood latched onto it from Fernando Wood, a New York City mayor who proposed it in 1861—all of which buoys the Hemingway literary canon that good writers never plagiarize, they steal.

But all these men had proposed the idea for the financial benefits it would bring to the city. Mailer, as usual, took it further. He felt that New Yorkers were spiritually as well as financially bankrupt. And by going through the process of acquiring statehood, they would have a rebirth, a rediscovery of the soul.

He talked of the magic that would appear in New Yorkers as they were called upon to draft a constitution in convention, a convention peopled by Blacks, whites, and Puerto Ricans full of passion and heat tempered by cool logic, which would result in an instrument that would allow New Yorkers to live again.

As he talked, one recalled the remark Gene McCarthy made to him many years ago after hearing him deliver a speech at a New York party: "Better learn how to breathe, boy." Though many in the audience were intrigued, the veil of practicality began to cloud their faces. Swashbucklers on the high political seas may be romantic, but in the last reel the adherents to parliamentary procedure always prevail.

When he launched into his concept for Black control—control of their schools, police, and, indeed, their economy, his voyage came to an end. A young woman, who must have done a case study of Brett Ashley (floppy hat, cigarette holder, *et al.*), stood and served her words with a chill that shocked, similar to one's first taste of vichyssoise: "Mr. Mailer, your function is to create better programs for *them*, not to give *them* control."

Mailer tried to recoup by stating that self-government was essential, that abstract government is what has created the malaise of Western civilization. Then a middle-aged woman, crowned by a pillbox hat (her fortress of respectability), her shoulders a field of furry little foxes, cried: "Oh, no, that's not how the people I know think."

A rebellious voice tried to come to Mailer's aid, but the parliamentary gavel fell, and the practical voice said: "Time is running short and the club has other speakers to hear from."

As Mailer left, he received a covey of civilized handshakes, signed a few autographs, and was rendered that bloodless encouragement fair-minded referees find it their duty to offer all combatants. It was all very civilized, all very polite, precisely the way Christians have been treating lepers for centuries.

The lesson wasn't lost on Mailer. The following evening he was scheduled to appear at the Lexington Democratic Club on East 86th Street in Manhattan. In the holier-than-thou reform circles, the Lexington Club prides itself on a purity second only to St. Theresa. It was the club that backed Republican Kenneth Keating against Robert Kennedy in their 1964 Senate race, because "Kennedy was an invader." Its members not only take pride in backing legislative bills but also find jabberwockian delight in being able to refer to the bills' sponsors: Weiss-Katzman Rent Control Bill, Mitchell-Lama Housing Bill. It also sponsors a youth movement that is so zealous it would have won acclaim in Berchtesgaden.

Mailer entered the long rectangular room, cased the crowd, and realized there was no payday here for him. Badillo buttons were on every jacket and dress to give fair warning to the trespasser. A bevy of young lawyers and emancipated women—*Redbook*'s young mamas, aggressive East Side swingers looking financially and sexually for room at the top, and the grande dames of good government who went to war for Stevenson and have been in uniform ever since—sat rigid on folding chairs, propped up by their expertise.

A middle-aged man engaging in peace games held the floor. He argued that a motion on the floor to recall all American troops from South Vietnam was out of order, since *he* had made the same motion three months before, and it had been recorded in the minutes. The chairman bowed to the original architect of withdrawal and began to introduce Mailer.

The introduction was one thing Mailer wasn't ready for. The chairman, a rather shapeless blond man, began speaking with an incredible lisp. We looked at each other, presuming we were witnessing an elaborate put-on. We weren't. After citing some of Mailer's literary accomplishments, he ended with a nervous giggle: "... and author of the current best seller, *Portnoy's Complaint.*" The climax was lost on Mailer.

Taking the line of direct attack, Mailer began: "What wonders to behold—to find such a brood in one place." But this was only a playful jab to set them up where they were most vulnerable, right in their ever-loving reform. For this was the club that backed Robert Wagner's third-term bid for mayor against "the bosses," a bid many political analysts felt was Kafkaesque, since Wagner was running against himself. And now the once golden champion was so much dross to be ignored, moreover, to be forgotten like a youthful indiscretion.

Mailer remembered. "I'm delighted to meet the club that made a reformer out of Robert Wagner," he said. In retaliation they rose even stiffer in their seats, jutting their Badillo buttons into clear view like crucifixes to ward off this raiser of dead memories.

Mailer was not about to quit when he was ahead. He spoke about the benefits the fifty-first state would bring: "We would save the mayor his annual embarrassment of going to Albany and getting on his knees to kiss Governor Rockefeller on the mouth."

A small squadron in the back of the room formed an attack on Mailer. His proposition was ridiculous. Why should Albany agree to allow the city to cut itself free if, indeed, in Mailer's estimate the city was a huge source of income for the state?

Mailer countered with an explanation of the legal procedures to achieve statehood: a Mailer victory, a constitutional convention, passage by the state assembly in Albany of the new state's constitution, then on to ratification by the Congress of the United States.

But all this was politely dismissed. Why should Albany ever ratify such a move, even if Mailer carried out a miracle of DeMille dimension by winning? Mailer was losing ground on their legal battlefield, so he decided to shift to his own terrain.

Employing the accent of an Albany farmer, or what he imagined was the accent of an Albany farmer (Who the hell was knowledgeable enough to dispute it?), he said: "Well, those farmers up there might want to get rid of all us evil Jews and niggers." Well, the farmers' desires aside, Mailer managed to get rid of his audience, and quickly. With a frenzied, flapping movement, they flocked to the back of the room—a collective tsk tsk.

Out on the street, Mailer realized he had lost the war but won the battle: "No matter what I said to them, they would have been against me. So I decided to give it to that pack of plastic cunts."

The next morning Steinem found a headquarters on 58th Street at Columbus Circle, and we were ready to hang out our shingle. The headquarters had the dual advantages of a prominent location on the circle and familiarity to volunteers, since it had been the site of the McCarthy-O'Dwyer operation. But the familiarity also brought a melancholy, for it was here that the young marshaled their near-miracle, only to have the reverse alchemy of the delegates' arithmetic and the nightsticks of the Chicago cops reduce their magic to a dull reality. But it was available, and we were badly in need of a home.

Since sad reverie is the province of the old, our fear was unfounded—the young came again. Under Bina Bernard, a magazine editor and wife of Walter Bernard, the art director of *New*

York magazine, a nucleus started to form. Bina proved ideal to head up the office operation, for so far the campaign was inundated with broad strategists, generals, and would-be generals —all Rommels with spectacular objectives on the horizon and supply lines nowhere in sight. And like so many young professional women in the city, she was fiercely competent; but unlike many of her breed, she was a warm, generous girl to whom the young volunteers readily responded.

Among the first to come were David and Dale Weinstein. Dave, a slight, twenty-four-year-old teacher from Newark's Black elementary schools, has an air of sadness that manifests itself in sloped shoulders seemingly fixed in a perpetual shrug and a droopy mustache weary beyond its years. But the melancholy aura never affected his work. He was a tireless recruiter and handler of volunteers, continually moving across the floor from one duty to another or patiently mothering a constantly whining mimeograph machine. His wife, in oriental fashion, silently followed him about, gathering the loose ends of his labor and coordinating them into a final fixed arrangement.

Joining the Weinsteins was Fred Weisner, a student at CCNY, recently discharged from the Army; but though his round baby face was covered with a manly beard, it was difficult to think of him as a veteran. Bill Cobb, a young writer newly arrived in New York from Boston and the father of two girls, who spent his nights as a hotel clerk and his days as a volunteer, rounded out the initial group. So, with Steinem working on fund raising and Krakauer on scheduling and this small band to which Mailer would refer as "his hearties," the campaign started to roll.

On Tuesday, the twenty-second, Breslin joined the campaign trail. The first stop of the day was to have been City College, but because of turmoil on the campus, we canceled our appearance. The revolution taking place on college campuses was to prove a major consideration throughout the campaign. For we were soon to realize we were not tilling the same fertile fields that Gene McCarthy found, where the crop of peace was waiting to be harvested. After Chicago, wild weeds started to grow and flourish at individual colleges: open admissions policies, Black and Third World study centers, and administrative equality. So, unlike McCarthy, who dealt with a unified community, Mailer and Breslin had to appeal to baronies, each with its individual structures, suspicions, and intrigues, insulated from the "outside world"—all, in the vernacular of the times, "doing their own thing."

With the cancellation at CCNY, St. John's University in Queens was the first stop—hardly a place to begin a revolution. St. John's, a Catholic school with 13,000 students, had in the past matriculated in political conservatism. In straw polls, its students elected Barry Goldwater for President in 1964 and William F. Buckley, Jr., for mayor of New York in 1965. The student body is mainly of Irish and Italian descent, sons of the working class (dockworkers, transit workers, and minor civil servants), who will leave behind them the jaunty gray working caps of their fathers and don the fedoras of respectability when they enter the Protestant and Jewish world of Wall Street upon receiving their degrees in business administration.

There also is a segment of Jewish students who attend the University's law and pharmaceutical schools, but they are regarded as neither smart enough nor rich enough to achieve Harvard, so for all intents and purposes they, too, are considered *goyim*.

About 200 students gathered in Marrillac Hall, a pleasant, modern auditorium painted pale green, a color more alive and shades lighter than the dismal one used in the hallways of the old parochial schools throughout the city—a tribute to modern motif or perhaps to Pope John's airing of Catholic doctrine.

But the students' faces were a timeless catechism. One recalled the faces of his boyhood, with complexions pink as from a nun's slap. Their history was familiar and unchanging. These were the same kids who shot baskets at netless hoops in the blacktop schoolyards of Our Lady of Something or Another, who spent their summers on the "Catholic Rivieras" of Rockaway or the Jersey shore drinking flat pitcher beer and lindying to sounds that are now sociological relics. The girls were as pretty and as innocent as ever—their fine legs destined to grow heavy with too many children too early and their faces not able to comprehend the peculiar, parochial sexual complexity of compliment and insult: "You're too nice a girl to touch."

Breslin mounted the stage with an easy confidence, for he was part of them and at home among them.

The wayward son who had ventured outside his neighborhood began telling them of streets littered with criminals and dope addicts while city officials sit in the municipal building watching the clock. His credentials, he went on, had been earned in the streets, at the police stations, and on the rooftops of the city, "not in the Urban Studies Center at Harvard" (deftly turning with an apologetic smile to Mailer for denigrating his alma mater).

A girl not wanting to appear square asked him if he would legalize pot. Breslin, a natural actor, blustered like a bishop: "Do you go to St. John's? Where's the father? What kind of a crowd did we draw here?" He concluded by telling a story about the death of his grandmother in Ireland. According to Breslin, she was lying in her bed with a 50–50 chance for survival when a member of the family decided it was time to fetch "the poor woman the crucifix." Unable to find a small replica of the relic, the zealot took a large crucifix off the wall (an object that took on more poundage every time Breslin retold the story) and laid it on the poor woman's chest, crushing the last breath of life out of her. Breslin concluded: "My grandmother is the only woman I know who was killed by the Holy Cross."

Mailer, always the smooth assayer of military situations, realized this was Breslin's terrain and didn't try to seize the high ground. He spoke about achieving statehood, giving power to the neighborhoods, and allowing the left and right to seek their own life styles. The kids, looking for some practicality with the poetry, quizzed Mailer on the mechanics of such moves. Since the ideas were still in the stage of romantic notions, rather than firm programs, Mailer had a difficult time with the mechanics. Still, the ideas interested them.

A final question was addressed to both: "Are you really serious, or is all this a joke?"

Mailer grasped for an answer he couldn't find, but Breslin, assuming the unapproachable posture of an avenging angel, glared at his interlocutors: "Anyone who runs for office in this city, with the shape this city is in, and takes it as a joke is committing a mortal sin."

An embarrassed silence fell over the hall. It was as if one had questioned the intentions of Sir Thomas More. Whether his motive was political or spiritual, it was quite evident Breslin possessed untapped potential in the field of conversion.

The next stop of the day was Union Theological Seminary in upper Manhattan. During the car ride in from Queens, Breslin basked in his glory and criticized Mailer's performance. It was decided that they both should be more informed on the practical procedures of attaining statehood and neighborhood control.

They also debated the use of the slogan "Power to the Neighborhoods." Since neighborhood control in New York is synonymous with Black control, they wondered if the word "power" wasn't too strong, since to some it called up a military image—complete with borders, weapons, and defense of one's own turf, which was bad enough; but, moreover, would the good burghers of Queens and Staten Island next think of invasion? Breslin, enjoying a day of infallibility, came up with the notion of returning government to "the *wisdom* of the neighborhoods."

In its own way, Union Theological Seminary in the heart of upper Manhattan is as parochial as St. John's in docile Queens. The neo-Gothic seminary is far removed from the world that borders it—a monastic retreat tucked away in a foreboding forest of tenements, with hallways like treacherous paths which the misbegotten travel in their road to hell.

We walked through a pastoral quadrangle, where one expected to find young men strolling and reading vespers, to the hall in which Mailer and Breslin were to speak. On its rough white walls hung a gallery of pompous gents bedecked in flowing red robes. Candled chandeliers hung from the ceiling, casting light on chairs so overstuffed they seemed to wheeze. Sons and daughters of America's WASP aristocracy formed a crescent around the speaker's podium. And though Breslin's physiognomy suited the gouty motif, one wondered how his theology would be accepted in such a setting.

Indeed, at the beginning of his address it seemed as though the street genius would take his cap in hand and pander to his betters. He nervously mumbled that he was impressed and contrite to appear before such a collection of PhD's. Then his voice took on a gravelly confidence as he detailed his own education.

"I went to John Adams High School in Queens," he began, and after a proper pause added, "for five years."

"The school," he continued, "was located by the quarter pole at Aqueduct Racetrack. The first English sentence I ever learned was 'It is now post time.' They decided to build a wing on the high school," he went on, "and they had to move the quarter pole at the track. The moving of the quarter pole was the cultural high point in the school's history."

They were all his now, punctuating his every sentence with

their laughter. It was a stroke of political genius that Breslin was to perform on every campus. He made the students feel guilty for their formal education, their comfort, their world, and their experience which was bound neatly between covers. It was a feat Mailer could never attempt, even though his personal life was embellished by the bizarre. For Mailer was after all still middle class, Jewish, and Harvard, a reader of Blake, Lowell, and Kierkegaard, and so to be regarded as one of their own.

But Breslin's confidants couldn't be found in the Dewey decimal system, if they were to be *found* at all. One would have to understand the intricacies of the police blotter to discover Mutchie, Fat Thomas, and Marvin the Torch.

Breslin next spoke of his graduating class: "We produced sixteen New York City policemen, seventeen New York City firemen, and thirty-two of the most prominent felons in this city." And after the laughter died: "And seventy-five body and fender men who were open to any proposition."

He then told them that there was only one issue here—the issue of Black and white, and "Robert Wagner, who came into town last week like a busted valise, isn't going to settle it." He predicted civil war in the city if we failed to try something new, with New Yorkers ending up "with shotguns on Park Avenue." He reached his conclusion and, probably deciding that the evocation of mortal sin would be wasted on an audience of Protestants, looked out the window at the greenery, then chillingly observed: "You have a nice quadrangle here. You're going to need it."

Breslin's performance left a fine competitive edge in the air, and Mailer swaggered to the podium keyed for combat. When the invitation to appear had been extended, it was accompanied by a request that Mailer read from one of his works. "I was asked here for a reading," he began, "and I didn't want to offend either politics or literature—so I will pay homage to both." Then, smiling: "Politics first."

Mailer remarked why he was eminently qualified to be a politician: "I can look without horror upon any man whose hand I have to shake. The difference between me and the other candidates is that I'm no good, and I can prove it."

Realizing that the street was Breslin's domain, Mailer left the gutters behind and led them to the mountaintop. In a quiet voice he explained that it was a spiritual necessity to give vent to the ideas of both the left and the right: "People are healthier if they live out their prejudices rather than suppressing them in uniformity."

He proceeded to take them on a tour of America's spiritual wasteland, stopping along the way for commentary on our alienation, racism, technological madness, and impotence. It was a performance of miraculous proportions. The audience sat in ecclesiastical reverence as he did that of which only he was capable—convincing a collective body that the sadness in his soul was symbolic of the sadness in the land, that his personal tragedies weren't encased in his psyche but wrapped in a shroud of red, white, and blue. For the first time since we began, I erased the practical arithmetic in my brain and swore to Christ that Norman Mailer was going to become the mayor of New York City.

He took them to the brink of the apocalypse, but never over the edge. When he dealt with the question of law, he mixed profundity with glee. "My notion of the law as written," he said, "is that it was conceived to catch every whore and make every mean man rich." The reason that Robert Wagner's entry into the primary was being applauded, he intoned, was that "Robert Wagner is a magnificent Seeing Eye dog who can lead us through the legal thicket of New York's city charter"; and that "the

Honorable Bob is the past master of confrontation under the table."

In conclusion, he said that he and Breslin would bring their message to "Protestants, Catholics, Black Muslims, and, occasionally, charming atheists."

For a peroration they asked him to read his description of the Republicans at Miami from his book on the national Presidential conventions, *Miami and the Siege of Chicago*. As his verbal whip stung the Republicans for their Bible Belt piety, suburban sickness, and loss of the real Christ, the Protestants collected in the audience writhed in a masochistic delight usually experienced only in unspeakable houses in such unnatural outposts as Tijuana.

When Mailer concluded, a young man at the back of the room asked if he would accept the presidency of the seminary should his mayoral bid fail. "By electing me president," he replied, his voice bloating with mock pomposity, "you would bring much honor to the Jews."

They stood together at the podium as the audience rose in a boisterous standing ovation which shook the delicacy of the hallowed hall. It was then, with no small pride, that I realized I was handling the most balanced ticket in town: Mailer rose to the occasion; Breslin lowered himself to it.

To round out an ecumenical day Mailer was to appear that evening before a group of reform Democrats at the Menora Temple in the Boro Park section of Brooklyn. Breslin took the night off, a pattern that would develop during the campaign. He was a firm believer that conversion should take place under God's sunshine, reserving the nights for self-baptism in many of the city's watering holes.

Mailer and I were driven to Brooklyn by a young volunteer from Yale, John Saylor, one of many who would opt for the duty of driving the candidate on his daily schedule. Before going to the temple, we ate in Michel's restaurant, a Brooklyn landmark on Flatbush Avenue. Mailer recalled eating there when he was a boy and thinking it was the ultimate in class. The years didn't seem to have diminished his enthusiasm. He talked fondly of Brooklyn; its people were "real people," not like those "fuckin' phony liberals in Manhattan."

He rambled on about the fun he was having getting out into the neighborhoods and the growing respect he was beginning to feel for the people. One sensed that after years of working isolation, interrupted by hobnobbing with the rich and the talented, Mailer was rediscovering his city and enjoying it. To him his campaign was like Steinbeck's *Travels with Charley*.

The hall in the Menora Temple where the meeting was being held is one of those decorative wonders peculiar to Brooklyn and Queens, a blend of Miami Beach and Mafioso. The walls are covered with red flocked paper which, with the subtlety of a cymbal, collides with the black and red carpet, all catching the glitter of the plastic Versailles chandeliers. And so the red wouldn't be overdone (or, in the vernacular of the neighborhood, make the room "too busy"), the windows are covered in white like cadavers. Further, to give credence to the old saw that a tree grows in Brooklyn, plastic palms dot the room, unperturbed by the harsh lights, the cigar butts, and the flat scotches which through the years have served as fertilizer—nonliving monuments to Nature, just what God would have done if he'd had the right decorator.

Since other candidates also were scheduled to speak, Mailer was allotted eight mintues to make his pitch. He outlined his basic program and embroidered it with "Sweet Sunday." Sweet Sunday was to be one Sunday a month when all traffic in the city would be banned, including outgoing and incoming planes and all ships at sea. In addition, all power would be shut off, except for generators in hospitals (a qualification Mailer made when he was accused of programming genocide for the feeble).

So, in a moment of unprecedented political dash, Mailer lost the votes of the subway and elevator riders, the devotees of air conditioning, frozen food, washers, and dryers, and that pampered breed of male who conquers his stubble with an electric razor. But all was not lost. On the positive side, he won undisputed acclamation among the city's numerous hippies, all of whom thought the electoral process was irrelevant.

Mailer spoke quickly and then opened the floor to questions. What would happen if he was elected? "Washington would fall to its knees."

What was the advantage in divorcing the city from Albany? "You will admit it will take less time to travel to our money."

And finally, what would happen if his Sweet Sunday went into effect? "On the first hot day the populace would impeach me."

In the best show-business tradition he left them laughing and buoyantly headed for Manhattan to meet Breslin at campaign headquarters, where an official opening at which the candidates were to greet the volunteers was scheduled. At headquarters Mailer and Breslin mounted a table to talk to about 200 volunteers, most of them kids. Mailer, physically tired and obviously tired of repeating the litany of his platform, wasn't very effective. He took precautions to be gentle with the other candidates, especially Badillo. The young who had come out into the night looking for a rebellious rising of the moon were in no mood for Marquis of Queensbury politics.

Breslin, a descendant of those who held their nighttime brawls on barges with bare knuckles, knew better. After welcoming the volunteers to the cause, he summed up the opposition in his own inimitable fashion. "They're all a bunch of shit heelers," he roared as the young let up a rebel yell.

In the car ride back to his home in Brooklyn, Mailer rested his head on the back of the seat, exhausted after his day. It had been the first of many sixteen-hour days candidate Mailer would put into his attempt to capture City Hall.

From mid-April into May, Mailer was the most active candidate in town. He spoke at seventeen colleges during this period and accepted every speaking engagement tendered by Democratic clubs and civic groups. Much of the sloth of the other candidates was due to the machinations or lack of them on the part of Robert Wagner.

After his formal announcement on April 11, Wagner remained silent for two weeks on who would fill out his ticket. Congressman Carey withdrew from the mayoral race, while the Democratic boss of his native Brooklyn, Meade Esposito, maneuvered to get him the second spot on the Wagner slate.

Norman Frank, a dapper gray-haired man given to wearing shiny suits and speaking with French-cuff finesse, the epitome of squad-room class, was public relations counsel for the Patrolmen's Benevolent Association and an early law-and-order candidate. On Wagner's entry, he resigned to back Procaccino, the founder of his three-word philosophy.

Congressman John Murphy of Brooklyn also threw in the sponge; and former City Council president Paul Screvane, whose entry into the race was as brief as the flicker of a candle, joined the Wagner campaign staff.

So, for the moment, the race narrowed down to those Wagner couldn't yet buy or scare off: Procaccino was in to the death; Scheuer while his checkbook held out, presumably for eternity; Badillo was a potential dropout, if Wagner offered him the spot for City Council president (that is, if the latter wanted to add some young, reform dynamism to the ticket to offset John Lindsay's star quality in November); and the strangely motivated long-distance runner, Norman Mailer. So, as Mailer engaged in an all-out assault on the electorate, the others were content to sit back and observe Robert Wagner maneuver, an art as exciting as watching the 1966 Chicago White Sox trying to bring a man in to score from second base, a process equal, according to their manager, Eddie Stanky, to "watching paint dry."

The final week in April was cyclonic with exhilarating ups and dead-end downs. The spirit at the colleges generally ran high, but the press began to nag the candidates, the general criticism being that "Mailer and Breslin is a joke." In the conservative New York *Daily News*, their bid was a barroom gag of the left. To the liberal *Times* and especially to the *Post*, it was a dangerous, insidious exercise that could produce a conservative mayor by splitting the vote of the liberal community.

The column that particularly stung Mailer appeared in the New York *Post*, written by editor and columnist James Wechsler and titled "The Odd Couple." Wechsler's complaint was odd in itself: it bothered him to no end that Mailer *was* taking the race seriously. So the liberal press was actually of two minds: Mailer should approach the race with the sobriety of a hanging judge; or conversely, Mailer should become a left-wing gadfly, à la William Buckley, Jr. But what particularly cut Mailer about Wechsler's column was the "odd couple" reference. He saw it as a smack at his manhood, which was not to be treated gayly by a liberal columnist.

But these snipes were inevitable. There was little compatibility between the liberal mind and Mailer's. A smallness of spirit had solidified itself in the liberal breast, partially diminished by lack of triumph. Many liberal heroes and causes had been leveled by the great American middle. But more, it was because liberals have no passion for their cause. The mother lode of their defense is loyalty, the loyalty that stems from nostalgia, not from reality. They were forced to cherish a dream that had failed. So Mailer's exercise confounded them. He was exposing himself to all comers; he was putting his secure literary reputation on the very fickle line of a voting booth, and since there was no way to hedge his bet, it was a gamble they couldn't understand. For intellectually and morally, they were loan sharks; and Mailer was a drunken high roller, a profound difference they never would grasp.

The attacks from the press establishment proved a blessing in disguise on the rebelling campuses, and Mailer and Breslin milked them to the hilt. Mailer told audiences that Wechsler "hasn't had a new idea since toilet training." And Breslin, a former *Post* columnist, raged at the paper for having placed his past prose "among the girdle ads" and flatly stated that if Ernest Hemingway had written for the *Post*, he never would have been discovered. The *Daily News* was below Breslin's lofty contempt. He accused the paper of carrying on a cultural exchange program with the International Longshoreman's Association—a job swap between reporters and dockworkers, with dockworkers (according to Breslin) receiving a royal screwing. And any student who dared to mention the phrase "the odd couple" to Mailer got a recitation of the multiple moral perversions in which Wechsler engaged with numerous publishers and editors, thus establishing him as an authority on odd coupling.

About this time an underground paper called *Screw* ran a story written by a female reporter giving her imagined evaluation of the mayoral candidates' prowess in bed. Mailer was portrayed as a lover with muscular thighs and buttock-enveloping hands and the possessor of a lightning rod that unleashed thunderclap orgasms. From the smile on his face as he read the piece, it was easy to envision which paper would first be brought to the new mayor over breakfast coffee at Gracie Mansion.

It was during this week that I urged Mailer to announce his candidacy. Our petition drive was going poorly, and I felt a formal announcement might give us a boost. Reports from the canvassers indicated that many people wouldn't sign a petition for a clandestine challenger. Besides, all this sitting back gave the campaign a rather precious aura of "I'll materialize if the city beckons." Mailer agreed, and we decided to announce on the first day of the month—May Day.

In an all-out effort to line up volunteers before their announcement, the candidates made a final blitz of the colleges. At Columbia, a tough, radical audience sat silently while Mailer laid out his platform. Disaster was averted when an old Mailer enemy, technology, became an ally. The microphone into which he was speaking started to let out whines of interference, the trouble coming from the control booth in the back of the hall. Mailer bashed the instrument aside and shouted in the direction of the darkened control booth to an unseen, shadowy tormentor: "Where are you, fuckface?" The radicals, with their special knowledge that the real enemy is somewhat like the Loch Ness monster—rumored but unsubstantiated—roared their approval. And, having hit the right note, Mailer played it out. He told them that disruption is more authentic than walking around like a high-grade concentration-camp victim. He then took a smack at the "petite bourgeoisie," a tactic that is as effective among radicals as baby-kissing among mothers. Mailer was learning.

Another day began at Brooklyn College, a mannerly, liberal, predominantly Jewish institution that of late, because of the growing number of Black students on campus, had had some mild flirtations with radicalism. Before Breslin spoke, a boy in the audience told him that he must denounce a teacher who was present as a racist, or he would not be allowed to speak. Breslin instructed the Young Turk to shut the hell up and sit down. Down he sat, and the revolution was over.

Then Mailer, in the midst of a nostalgic valentine to the departed Brooklyn Dodgers, was interrupted by a young man whose mind was on winter sports, namely, snow removal. "What would you have done about the snow in Queens?" he asked, referring to a heavy snowfall the previous winter that the Lindsay administration had been unable to remove in that borough for days. In no mood to have his sunny reverie of Whitlow Wyatt and Pete Reiser interrupted by such slush, Mailer let him have it. "I'd piss on it," he roared.

Mailer wasn't overly impressed with the student body. "The problem with these kids," he remarked, "is that they would rather jerk off at a beautiful thought than have a dubious fuck with a mean woman."

At Long Island University in the commercial district of Brooklyn, Breslin held forth on politicians and Brooklyn politics. "I'm not the brightest person in the world," he began, "but wait till you see those other bastards. Those guys say a publication like *Screw* is obscene. What the hell do they think a picture of a politician shaking hands with Martin Luther King is?" And always with emotion, his references to Robert Kennedy: "Every guy in the race is running around town saying he was anointed by Bobby Kennedy to be mayor. I'll tell you something. That little guy is trying to crawl out of the grave to choke those sons of bitches with his bare hands." Wherever he delivered this line, there inevitably was a young girl in the audience whose hand went to her mouth in confusion to muffle either a laugh or a sob.

They began to discover each other's style and complement it. Breslin would cite corruption on street corners: "The Mafia runs Brooklyn politics. And, believe me, they're not an Equal Opportunity employer." Mailer would handle the shady doings in the sky: "The alternative is to drift on to more smog, hopelessness, and shit." There was a subtle class distinction: Jimmy would handle the cops and crooks; Norman, being too well bred and too well educated to know about such things, would combat the cosmos.

Every performance got better. Breslin would come on first,

loosen them up with laughs, and then plunge them into the gutter of despair. Mailer, like the ever reliable cavalry, would come to the rescue, his voice a spiritual bugle bearing wings for their abject spirits.

One also began to notice another trait. James Breslin was a ham of goodly proportion. He was always the first to tell anyone who would listen how casually he was taking the race—he was out "taking a walk around," he would say; but come each new day, Breslin had a new line prepared to add to his repertoire, a treat Mailer and I anxiously awaited. He also had a built-in laugh meter. If a line went well at an early stop, it traveled with him all day; but if it failed him, it would receive a morning burial, never to be heard again.

He delivered his masterpiece at New York University. Gloriously hung over from the night before, he was in rare form. Mailer, a victim of that same sad disease of the night, had shown up wearing a plaid sports jacket with solid pants and a white dress shirt open at the neck. Breslin couldn't have been more delighted: "This is the way it should be—both of us hung over, you dressed like a detective in those fuckin' Seventeenth Precinct clothes. Just the way it should be."

Breslin never missed a news story if he could, as in this instance, make hay out of it. The morning papers reported that the backstretch employees at Aqueduct Racetrack had gone out on strike in their fight to obtain a pension fund. So Breslin began: "The only reason I'm here is that the racetrack is closed because of the strike." Taking a breather, he added: "Jesus, the SDS is closing everything down."

A young man who was wary of Celtic charm asked him if, indeed, he just wanted to become another Jimmy Walker, to which Breslin retorted: "I wish I had his broads." He went on to hatchet-murder the opposition in his usual humane fashion. But when Wagner's turn came, he paused to savor the handiwork that was before him; then: "Robert Wagner is so attuned to the times that the first person he called for support when he got back to the city was Cardinal Spellman."

Columnists and barflys quoted him, and Murray Kempton was so moved by what he found to be the political profundity of the remark that he endorsed Breslin in his column. Of course, there also were those who were offended by his irreverence for a dead cardinal and a recently resurrected politician, but the point was that they had heard the line. For a slight season two campaigners, James Breslin and Douglas MacArthur, had in common the majesty of their quotes.

But Breslin's glory was to be short-lived. He would suffer a humiliating defeat at the hands of the female supremacists at Sarah Lawrence College. When we arrived from the city, our first glimpse of the gentle, green campus gave no indication of what was to come. Young girls in shorts walked barefoot through the grass, and one had the feeling an easy victory could be achieved in such a pastoral setting. Precisely the same feeling, one supposed, the Redcoats had the first time they encountered the Iroquois.

It was bad from the beginning. Breslin opened with something to the effect that he would have completed his education had he known so many pretty young girls went on to college. Nothing. He next mentioned that his wife was glumly enduring his foray into political life. The domestic image got him less than nothing. He had a standard line about politicians leaving the younger generation a legacy of "shit," but today he said he wouldn't use the word in deference to their sex. It was a miscalculation as awesome as Custer's. Shrieks of "male chauvinist" filled the room. "Say it," they shouted, "say it." Breslin, completely routed, meekly said: "Shit."

The leader of the faction was a girl with a long straight mane of brown hair which she constantly tossed out of her eyes in the best Bette Davis tradition. "The question, Breslin," she sneered, "is what are you going to do with the imperialistic dogs like Chase Manhattan and Con Edison?" Breslin tried to get out of it by commenting that even his wife didn't address him that way. "All right, James," she said, stretching the "James" as though she had it on a rack, "the question is what would you do with the imperialists?" Breslin looked like he'd never loved his Rosemary more.

Mailer attempted to rescue him and nearly succeeded. He began by saying his campaign was a military assault: brilliant, imaginative, and Napoleonic, and he reminded them that there had been very few Napoleons. So far, so good. He then expressed his theory of power to the neighborhoods, a turf for every lifestyle. The razor-straight hair flashed again and in a voice that would make the Washington Monument go limp, the girl demanded: "Where are the pigs going to live?" Mailer made the mistake of putting on his whiskey baritone Rhett Butler accent to reply. "Look, sugar," he began, and got no further as a chorus attacked him for the endearment.

There was no tactic left but open assault, and Mailer took it. He called them a left parliament and said that as long as there was one good cop in twenty, the lady was making the mistake of her life in calling all policemen "pigs." She countered with: "Power to the Neighborhoods is an empty slogan." Mailer shot back that she was a Marcusean and a totalist, and Breslin chimed in that while she was worrying about Chase Manhattan and South Africa, we were losing Brooklyn. Mailer successfully reached for a parallel and won the final round. "Lenin once had a slogan," he said: "Power to the Soviets."

Outside in the car, Breslin pathetically tried to salvage a victory: "Norman, you gave them that high-class Harvard shit. I should go back in there and call them a bunch of dumb dike cunts." But no one really wanted to go back in, and everyone was grateful when the car pulled away. Whatever we may have lost inside, we decided, wasn't vital; or at least we hoped not, since nobody had yet mustered enough courage to check.

Newfield and Gorman, who had been in Puerto Rico for a week, returned, and we held a staff meeting at Steinem's. The first order of business was money. Our war chest currently consisted of $600, and there were no large contributors on the horizon.

Laird Cummings, a former campaign coordinator for Manhattan Congressman William Ryan, ran down probable campaign expenses in a weary fashion and casually estimated we would need between $50,000 and $75,000. Mailer, instead of being shocked by the figure, seemed to enjoy the estimate. It gave his campaign a professional air. So far, it had been financed by Mailer and from small contributions we received in response to the ads in the *Village Voice*. Breslin, who continually promised a large check from some shadowy contributor, once again stalked out into the night to track down his elusive benefactor.

Cummings, a small man with owlish eyes and a voice on the far side of ennui, next ran down a list of paid staff members necessary to run a campaign, including his own position and salary. One began to suspect he was a mean man with *Robert's Rules of Order*.

Gorman then took the floor in an emotional outburst and charged that the campaign was not moving, a charge I didn't take kindly from someone who had just returned from a week of sun and fun in Puerto Rico. But I had a nice feeling for Gorman and thought that he was undergoing a bad personal period, perhaps because of the McCarthy campaign. He was to drop out of the campaign after this meeting, returning only once to give Mailer advice on an impending television debate.

The general feeling at the meeting was that it was time for

the revolution to "get respectable," so we went the way of all purists and formed committees. Newfield and Maas were to be the press secretaries; Stokes, Linzer, Friedman, and Ferris would handle petitions; Stu Sosler, a stockbroker and friend of Cummings', would head finance; Krakauer would continue with scheduling; and the office operation would remain under Bina Bernard and the Weinsteins. Jack Banning, a radio announcer and former State Department employee, who had helped advance Robert Kennedy's South American tours and who was present because of his association with Maas (he had interviewed Maas on his radio show), was hired as Mailer's advance man. Peter Manso, an English teacher at Rutgers who was currently writing a critical biography of Mailer, and Susan Harmon, a reform Democrat who specialized in urban problems, would handle research and drafting of position papers. Steinem, as Oscar Levant said of Zsa Zsa Gabor, was to continue her social work among the rich. Now we had not only a staff but a payroll to meet as well.

When the meeting broke, Mailer retired to the bathroom to write his announcement speech on a piece of gray cardboard of the type laundries use in packaging freshly ironed shirts. Then he went off to meet Breslin at a midtown saloon for dinner and drinks before heading to Brooklyn to speak to a group of reform Democrats who were giving a fund-raising party for the civil rights movement in Northern Ireland. Mailer told the boozy gathering he was running on a program of everything "from Black power to Irish self-righteousness."

On the eve of his announcement, Joe Ferris, my wife, and I joined Mailer at his home. Mailer, who was working on a piece for the Sunday *New York Times Magazine* section on why he was seeking office, was in high spirits after writing 5,000 words that day. His dress fitted the jauntiness of his mood: black and white checkered slacks and a blue blazer. And a goodly portion of gin helped maintain it.

He began to lay out broad strategies: the delivery of two position papers every week and walking tours in each of the boroughs. He expressed the feeling that his chance of winning the primary was a mere 6 to 1. One felt that Breslin would have loved to book the bet.

We were joined by Mailer's wife, Beverly, an earthy woman who, like Breslin's wife, would rather tend to the privacy of her home and children than get involved in the public limelight, and Lee Cook, a friend of Mailer's from Provincetown, who had appeared in Mailer's latest film. Cook is a lean, good-looking Black man with the elegance of an ebony walking stick. His every movement seems choreographed, his hands flutter like a bullfighter's cape with every verbal pass, and the adjustment of his ever-present sunglasses is a production number to behold. Mailer matter-of-factly introduced him as a "revolutionary," much in the same manner one would introduce another as a lawyer or as a plumber. Cook, relishing the role, pontificated on the ills of society and for the rest of the evening served as our guide to the dark continent. He offered a hip rendition of the Moynihan Report on the Black matriarchal society: "Black women are wary of all men; they think we're only out after their pussy." During his discourse, he would pause to remind us all that he was a "dialectical Marxist," and that the final solution lies in the murder of the white oppressors. Since Mailer was supplying the Beefeater gin Cook was drinking, I presumed he was to be spared.

I couldn't understand why Mailer would tolerate such gibberish, but during the course of the campaign I was to find out that he had a one-way love affair with street types. If someone had been part of an experience foreign to his own (being Black, a convict, a prizefighter), Mailer found in him occult powers bestowed only on the children of the gutters. Their dreariness of thought and total lack of performance in any function assigned to them made no difference to him. This enchantment had to do with Mailer's high sense of intrigue and his romantic notion of the streets. That the gutter was a spawning ground which produced dullness far more often than genius was never considered. It was a characteristic I found unattractive, similar to that of society broads who chase saxophone players and bouncers.

The following morning I picked up Mailer and Beverly at their house to drive them to the Overseas Press Club, a site of staid tradition I insisted on for the formal announcement, since I felt the candidates had to be decharismaized. Mailer got my message. He was dressed in his dark blue suit and vest, and his hair was trimmed and plastered down in regimental order. But his nerves were something else. He nagged me about my driving the entire way and was harsh with Beverly. When I gave him a reproachful look, he explained that he always beat up on his wife whenever he was nervous. It was a domestic exercise, he commented, that was good for both their souls. Since advice to the lovelorn was outside my managerial sphere, I remained silent and continued to drive.

When we arrived at 10 A.M., Breslin was nowhere in sight, and none of the staff had heard from him. I began to have visions of Rosemary's having strapped him to his bed. We waited another half hour. Still no sign of Breslin. The assembled press were growing restless, so we decided to proceed without him, announcing that he was on his way but trapped in traffic in Queens. The television cameras began to grind, and Mailer threw his hat into the ring in high literary fashion.

"We were warned yesterday that political campaigns were won at the last moment by the candidate who had the most money to spend on commercials. It was our thought that the candidates had become a little like the products put out by corporations. They were so similar that it took a commercial to purvey them.

"Well, Breslin and myself were not manufactured in large corporations. We were, in fact, put together by piecework. And if you wish to look at us as products, then think of us as antiques. Because we are sentimental about the past. We want New York to thrive again. We want New York to be a city famous around the world again for the charm, ferocity, elegance, strength, calm, and racy character of our separate neighborhoods.

"We are here to run a campaign and try to win on the idea that New York's problems are not her own—that we New Yorkers are victims of the governmental delusion that profound social problems can be solved from above. We believe poor people must be given the money and tools to solve their own problems their own way, and that all people are entitled to live in neighborhoods which correspond to their idea of how to begin a good life. So we are for increasing the city budget, rewriting the city charter, and giving power out to the neighborhoods, power back to the neighborhoods where power began. And for the instrument of this triple play we say that the first key to the first lock on the windpipe of this city is to separate from New York State and become a city-state.

"We are running on that. Our election in the Democratic primary would be magic. Our election in the mayoralty election would be a miracle. But if we are elected, we will be ready to say that the people of New York have given Mailer and Breslin a mandate to set us on the route to a city-state. On that day you may decide if we are serious or not.

"Gentlemen, we are ready for your questions."

Before questions started, the television cameramen asked Mailer to stand on a box so that his head would be clearly visible over the microphones on the podium. Mailer replied that the electorate would have to get used to a short mayor; and, besides, he would not deal in any deceptions, since his campaign slogan was "No More Bullshit."

The cameras started to whir in earnest now. Paying homage to television, Mailer repeated the slogan for the cameras making the necessary deletion. "Gentlemen," he said, "we are running on 'No More Beep-Beep.' "

On the second "beep" Breslin entered the room, confirming my worst suspicions. He was not accompanied by Rosemary, and his face looked like a ravaged battleground. His eyes, sunken into his head, obviously had been on guard duty all night in some saloon, and his voice croaked from whiskey and cigars. In cursory fashion he slandered the opposition and praised himself and Mailer, and then he concluded by saying that someone had warned him running for office would endanger his credibility as a writer. "I told him," he said, "it didn't hurt Winston Churchill."

Some poor reporter, obviously looking for color, asked Breslin if announcing on May Day had any significance. Breslin glared at him. Obviously having been outclassed at home, he finally had an opponent he could handle. He called the reporter "stupid"; he demanded to know his name and for what paper he worked. He went on to admonish every reporter in the room for not having given the Mailer-Breslin ticket, "the class of the field," the proper coverage. They were giving space instead to "those other idiots."

Mailer soothed things with a few ideological pleasantries on politics, and I gave him a signal to end the press conference while we still had the reporter from Tokyo on our side.

Outside in the street, Breslin couldn't be controlled. He heaped every obscenity known to man on the fourth estate: "Don't tell me, Norman, about those bastards, those pricks. I should know. I wrote the book. Ask my wife."

And finally, with our campaign less than a month old, we made the transition from revolutionaries to reactionaries, from the proletarian to the powerful, as Breslin solemnly said: "You know something, Norman? Mayor Daley was right about the fuckin' press."

3
Trying to Multiply the Fishes

A FTER their announcement, the candidates carried their crusade to the living room of the poetess Sandra Hochman on Manhattan's posh upper East Side, in quest of money. The fund raiser had been arranged by Steinem, and a glance at the collective frocks and rocks proved she had done her job well.

Paintings were hung strategically throughout the apartment, and in the living room stood a piano, keyboard open, with a piece of sheet music in the rack giving the hint that we might have interrupted a recital in progress.

The ladies present were a working boy's fantasy. Their bodies had a glorious idleness about them, as if they spent the better part of the time immersed in fine bath oils, and the skin of the one Black woman there seemed to be dusted with purple talc. Then there were the older ladies with crowns of small afternoon hats and creased turkey throats, gently cackling and comfortably nesting, while the younger chicks scurried around attending to the niceties.

In a foyer off the living room, coffee and cake were being served. Coffee is not exactly a commemorative beverage after the announcement of one's candidacy, but Mailer and Breslin faked enthusiasm. Not so for the New York working press, led by the *Times'* Sid Zion, who explored the pantry muttering: "Where's the fuckin' booze?"

Miss Hochman called Mailer into the living room to make his spiel. Coffee cup and saucer in hand, the pinky slightly extended, Mailer opened with a lead that was a sexual masterpiece. Realizing that the females gathered probably were apprehensive about confronting this much raw sexuality while it was still light, he gently began to mock his physical size. After all, he told them, he was just a small man with a limited ambition—the mayoralty—while John Lindsay with his greater stature and aspiration had his eye on the White House. It was a perfect ploy. They began to relax. They had come fearfully expecting a blustering Henry the Eighth, and much to their delight discovered a shy, stammering Henry Aldrich.

Breslin followed and kept his record with the distaff side clean. He was lousy. Where Mailer was gentle, evocative, and philosophical, Breslin just put his head down and charged with such lines as: "If things don't change, we're going to have shotguns on Park Avenue." This scare tactic created black thoughts of benign doormen with suspicious bulges under their knee-length coats, but Breslin, the proverbial bull in the china shop, kept butting away.

We had an engagement at Queens College, so we made our good-byes, leaving Steinem behind to collect the booty. Mailer, playing Ariel to Breslin's Caliban, performed a piece of saving magic at the door. Sandra Hochman, child in arms, stood surrounded by a covey of cooing females, and candidate Mailer without a blink deftly kissed his first baby.

When we arrived, Queens College was in a state of turmoil. White students were at war with the administration, demanding greater student control, and the Blacks were incensed over the cutback in a program offering admission to ghetto youths. The

SDS had seized one building, and Black students were wrecking the school's cafeteria.

About a thousand students sat in a sun-baked mall waiting for the candidates. Others sat or dangled from walls and windows, giving the campus the look of a seized border town. And then there was the heat and the flesh—young men, shirtless, with bodies that had not yet made the acquaintance of fat, and young girls in shorts whose brown thighs were covered with a veil of blond algae. And the shouts, the carnival yells of revolution. These were no pristine, cold ideologues, but a hybrid of radicals and bandits who felt that sweating, swearing, and screwing were weapons of the revolution.

As the candidates mounted the platform to speak, they roared. Following the usual pattern, Breslin moved forward first. But the kids were joyously shouting: "What about Nixon? What about the ABM? What about Daley?" Breslin stood waiting for them to quiet down. Finally, Mailer could no longer resist the compelling stink of sweat and sensuality. He put his arm across Breslin's body and pushed him aside, seizing the podium. And to answer all their questions and define their religion, he screamed, "Fuck!" plunging into them as if they were a pair of open legs.

Every politician has his kind of crowd. McCarthy preferred the cool, educated rationalists; Bobby Kennedy was at home with the disenfranchised, emotional Blacks; and this was Mailer's crowd—young, obscene, brazenly sexual, laced with physical daring. As he spoke and they responded, you felt like a voyeur as he wallowed in their collective heat.

A group of students invited the candidates into the seized building, and Mailer, now aroused beyond return, accepted— open to any proposition. Breslin meekly followed.

In an attempt to discourage more students from gathering on the seized fourteenth floor, the administration had shut down the elevator, so if one were going to join the revolution he would have to walk up fourteen flights of stairs. This condition was all the better for Mailer, the hater of machines, but Breslin, a creature of comfort, didn't look so happy.

The entrance to the stairway was guarded by a whiny young man being very officious about who was to be allowed to climb the stairs. He had the traditional look of all those young men who hover at the fringes of physical violence. One felt that when his radicalism diminished, he was destined to become the equipment manager of the football team. After a brief hassle during which the boy strangely yelled: "Let's have no violence," we started our ascent, Mailer leading the way.

On every landing there were handmade signs. HAD ENOUGH? THE REVOLUTION IS ONLY 10 FLOORS AWAY. Mailer attacked each stair as if it were a minion of the establishment and gave Breslin, puffing along behind and cursing his nocturnal habits, yet another cross to bear. The Harvard Mailer rubbed it into the streetcorner kid with taunts of "Are you still with me?" and "Come on, Jimmy, only eight flights to go." But if Breslin moved like a pack mule, he was just as stubborn and refused to quit under Mailer's taunts.

So, the steps became Zapata's mountain as Mailer, the urban revolutionary sans white horse, made for the summit with high-stepping élan.

When we reached the fourteenth floor, we were met by some students who directed us to the roof, where a larger group was surveying its conquest. Once again, Mailer beamed, and Breslin with Catholic stoicism picked up his burden and moved upward to the coronary that surely would crucify him a flight higher.

We climbed to the roof, and the candidates talked briefly with the students. Breslin's mind was on recapturing his wind and retreating to a civilized camp in the city where generals were wined rather than whipped, but Mailer carefully surveyed the terrain. Before him lay the borough of Queens, its landscape defiled by endless rows of expressionless apartment houses, a procession of zombies. In the distance stood Manhattan, melancholy in a shroud of smog. And high on this rooftop stood Mailer, an announced savior swelling with pure animal rage at the machines, the malaise, and the madness below. It was the noble savage against decadent Western civilization. All that was missing was Fay Wray and the airplanes.

The first two weeks in May were to be the easiest for me. My objective was singular—to get Mailer and Breslin on the ballot—and even though the petitioning initially wasn't going well, there was unity and high spirits at headquarters. Perhaps the reason for this was that realistically we believed placing them on the ballot was the only obtainable victory in the campaign. Too, as far as I was concerned, it was a task that past experience had prepared me to handle.

I decided to focus our petition drive on two boroughs, Manhattan and Brooklyn, since I felt they would be the boroughs most sympathetic to a Mailer-Breslin ticket. Staten Island was to be disregarded, since its residents' idea of a tolerable radical was the late Pope John. The Bronx and Queens, both geographically and politically, were a puzzlement to me. My forays into Queens were limited to Aqueduct Racetrack, and trips to the Bronx ended at Yankee Stadium. If residents or college students in these boroughs wanted to canvass their own area, fine; but no troops from the Manhattan headquarters would be sent to these distant hills.

It was a tactic that resulted in few adverse consequences during the petitioning, but it would prove harmful during the rest of the campaign. For if Mailer wished to unlock the windpipe of the city, he had made the unfortunate choice of a campaign manager who could play only two stops.

I took a leave of absence from the *Village Voice* to devote full time to the campaign. Mailer had offered me a lucrative salary; I declined because of our lack of funds and put myself on the payroll for the same weekly sum I collected from the *Voice*.

Our main problem with the petition drive was a lack of registered Democrats to collect signatures, since most of our volunteers were under twenty-one. Those who were of voting age were the city's political wine sniffers who kept their noses clean of machine and clubhouse aromas, so they might choose the choice bouquet presented; thus, they were registered Independents. The highest number of registered Democrats we ever had assembled on a given night was 22, a far cry from the number needed to obtain 15,000 signatures if we continued to use the traditional door-to-door method.

In a meeting with Friedman, Stokes, Linzer, Ferris, and a friend of Mailer's, Vinnie McGee, who had joined the petitions committee, we decided to scrap tradition and petition on key street corners in Manhattan and Brooklyn. The problem with this procedure was that it was open to challenge from another candidate on legal grounds. One of the reasons for collecting signatures in the voters' homes is that the law states the witness must be sure the signer lives at the address where he is registered to vote. On the street, if a prospective signer didn't carry his voter's registration card, you had no such assurance.

But to us the point was moot. It was a choice between following Grantland Rice's edict of "how you play the game" and morally nonproducing a noncandidate, or heeding Durocher's advice on where nice guys finish. We opted for Leo and hit the streets.

Ferris, who normally could weave solutions to knotty problems with the equivalent of a nail and a spool of thread, was frustrated by the petition drive in Brooklyn, because we were too broke to rent him a storefront. The Brooklyn operation was run out of hallways: Mailer's, mine, and any other kind soul's who would let us store card tables and chairs, signs, buttons, and blank petitions. So my annoyance with Ferris' inability to make do with what was given him was tempered by the realization that we had reduced our one saintly personality to conducting his business in Brooklyn hallways, a domain usually reserved for muggers.

On the brighter side, the office began to function professionally. Much of this new smoothness was attributable to Banning. It was easy to envision him as a valued employee of the State Department with his love of officialdom and dedication to detail. His makeup—red hair and goatee, dark blue business suit, and his ever watched wristwatch with a broad black leather band that looked like a perch for falcons—would mark him on Madison Avenue as one of the "new breed." And his voice was a masterpiece of diplomatic concern. Callers to headquarters were treated to such endearments as: "Of course, sweetie, I'll *personally* take care of it," while he constantly checked his watch as if he was dispatching bomber squadrons.

He and Mailer were instantly simpatico, for he rendered service hitherto unknown in our crude operation. Such touches as demanding the appearance of "the candidate's car" and leading Mailer through crowds with the slickness of a bribed maître d' gave the candidate endless delight. Banning's light blue eyes were his saving grace, the monitor of his many motions which mocked the pomposity of his performance.

Banning was assisted by his girlfriend, Sandra Elm, a small, blond woman-child who is not contemporary in the Lolita mold but nostalgically sexy—like those Kewpie dolls that graying Stage Door Johnnys used to shower with posies and bon-bons.

I also hired Laird Cummings as campaign coordinator, after convincing him that the spiritual experience of the campaign would be worth a reduction in his estimate of his material worth.

He would hold the office operation together on the days I went on the road with the candidates.

To assist Krakauer with scheduling, I hired Paul Tully, who had worked in that capacity for Allard Lowenstein during his successful 1968 bid for Congress. Tully, a huge, twenty-five-year-old Irish-American, is the son of a construction company owner and a graduate of Yale, where he received All-American honorable mention as a defensive tackle. Tully was a delightful breath of corrupt air in the heavenly atmosphere of the campaign. His first concern was not the malaise of the twentieth century, but how we were going to convince the Jews, who by far were the largest bloc vote in the primary, that Mailer and Breslin (like the Lone Ranger and Tonto) were the embodiments of law and order and still avoid offending horses of other colors.

Needless to say, Krakauer thought I had employed the services of the devil. Her concept of the campaign was to appeal, in her words, to the "cause people." Her scheduling list looked like a Bingo board: the Presidio 27, the Harlem 6, the Chicago 8. Tully's cold eye was on the arithmetic of the primary. It was an unhappy marriage from the beginning, with Alice constantly waving her handkerchief, like a flag of surrender, around her nose and eyes.

Something had to be done. Tully's point, that cause groups were naturally sympathetic to Mailer and constantly mining them would be a waste of time, was well taken. But Alice had been an industrious worker from the beginning and was a sensitive girl of fine instincts whose feelings I didn't want to hurt. A solution presented itself.

The press desk, which was supposed to be manned by Newfield and Maas, was going unattended. It had become clear that the role these two intended to play in the campaign was similar to the one Bobby Darin performed for Sinatra—Newfield and Maas wanted to play Mailer's prom dates. They joyously appeared on any television or radio show that the candidates couldn't handle or which they felt fell below their star quality. They also were the palace guard for the established left in the city and on occasion would spirit Mailer into the hallowed chambers of young Assemblyman Jerome Kretchmer or Steve Smith, the Kennedy brother-in-law. All such meetings did not appear openly on the schedule board, but cloaked in clandestine Pinter phrases like "Luncheon—private, address—unknown."

So, as Newfield and Maas engaged in their CIA work for the New Politics, Niles Peebles, a forty-one-year-old ex-reporter for the *Herald Tribune* who now made his living writing paperback mystery novels, was handling the press desk. And though he was capable of writing books with such ghoulish Dick and Jane titles as *See the Red Blood Run*, he was a gentle, considerate man who looked like a young Henry Fonda and seemed a perfect workmate for Krakauer. After some maneuvering, slight weeping, and declarations of love on all sides, Alice switched from scheduling to run the press desk with Peebles.

Tully, now free to dictate policy on scheduling, was joined by his wife, Heidi, a tall, magnificently legged girl at whom he would often stare admiringly and say: "I can't resist big jobs." Naturally, this convinced Krakauer that she had been right all along—Tully was without soul.

There were now six people, including me, on our payroll with salaries ranging from Banning's $175 per week top down to David Weinstein's weekly $50. One would guess it had to be the smallest payroll for a New York City mayoral candidate's staff in history; but then again, our critics would argue, what price glory? The hours extracted for the salaries were outrageous. Banning, Tully, and Weinstein averaged anywhere from twelve to sixteen hours a day, seven days a week, and their women frequently matched their hours for no pay at all.

Then there were the hard-core volunteers who held the day-to-day operation together: Gil Levine, a slight young man with shoulder-length hair, who worked in harness with Weinstein on overall office operations; Ronnie Rosner, a young mother who had fallen in love with Mailer's promise of "No More Bullshit" and entered her first campaign, taking charge of our financial records; Richie Fishman, a twenty-two-year-old Columbia graduate student in urban problems, was our student organizer on campuses, a function he had fulfilled for McCarthy in Massachusetts and New Hampshire; Meredith Sirna, a twenty-one-year-old student who had worked for McCarthy at Ohio University, and Angela Holdsworth, a friend of Krakauer's from Newcastle, England, now attending Tufts, became our receptionists. Angela's dignified British voice over the phone gave the campaign parliamentary dignity, and taking into account the average New Yorker's subservience to Mother England's master's voice, Angela just might have won us as many votes as our notion of the fifty-first state.

Spelling them at the desk was Jo Steinway, a middle-aged woman, industrious and practical, who looked at first glance as if she had the good sense to pass her time canning preserves instead of following the erratic stars of Mailer and Breslin. And then there was Morgan Godwin, our first conservative, the sperm of our hip left-right coalition. A bachelor in his late twenties, he attended NYU, where he was studying for his doctorate in political science. He formerly had backed Goldwater and Buckley but was now an ardent Mailer enthusiast because he found the candidate of his party, Staten Island state senator John Marchi, "too damn dull." He was not only inexhaustible but also imperturbable. He moved about headquarters checking out stacks of petitions with his tie at full mast and his hair, like the Red Sea, parted in divine order. He canceled a two-week fishing vacation to head a group responsible for checking all petitions for irregularities, a chore he managed with such crisp dispatch that he drove a deep dark fear, the unshakable canon of their mothers that "the neat shall inherit the earth," into the leftists. But through his hard work, he developed an ecumenism that led the shaggy revolutionaries lovingly to baptize him "Barry."

As we expanded, there were some minor brush fires to put out. Harmon and Manso, drafting our first position paper on air pollution, were as compatible as Krakauer and Tully. Harmon secretly husbanded her information sources from Manso, while he in turn demeaned her work to Mailer. Mailer, the proudly declared nonreader of Jane Austen (his bed badge of courage), was more sympathetic to Manso, a feeling that was strengthened when Harmon, uninvited, invaded a strategy session between the two at Mailer's home.

This problem of who was to have special access to the candidate's ear would prove troublesome throughout the campaign. I suppose it is a problem which plagues all campaigns, but when the infighting becomes bitchy, it's dangerous. Good minds and suggestions can be left standing outside the door, while inside a solitary voice is calling all the shots. I wasn't anxious to have Mailer end up with "his Pat Nixon."

But courting the candidate's ear was action in which I also indulged. The first time my opinion was not sought on an important matter, I was disturbed. Then I realized it was more than disturbance. Much to my blushing surprise, I pinpointed it as jealousy; but I was getting a little too old to learn to curtsy, so I decided to confine my energies to mapping broad strategies and running the staff.

Then there was the never-to-be-cured problem of advertising. Ten different agencies were offering their services, free of charge, to manipulate Mailer and Breslin. But who was to be chosen? Mailer, with what I thought was a straight face, suggested that representatives from all ten agencies meet at his home (together, no less) and bid for him as if he were an exotic slave girl. The suggestion was politely ignored until it was forgotten, and the jockeying for the account continued.

During this time, the printing of our handbills and flyers was handled by George Stonbely, a young man from Brooklyn on the make in the big city. He had worked in Bobby Kennedy's campaign, and his hustle suggested that his Syrian ancestors had been rug merchants to desert tent dwellers. Also in competition for the account was Kurtz and Kambanis, the agency that had handled Nelson Rockefeller's successful gubernatorial campaign. They were soon to learn that they would be better off confining their talents to aristocratic Protestants.

The sad part of all the account scrambling from the admen's viewpoint was that they would have no autonomy. Mailer wanted the final word on every project, and on the few occasions when he didn't have it, he was outraged. (Once, for good reason, when we spent $600 for posters and received a horrible mutation of what we'd ordered.) But on other orders, the minutiae were blown out of proportion. Any lettering that was embellished was "faggy" or "liberal"; and as the campaign wore on, the two terms (faggy, liberal) seemed to become synonymous to him.

When Stonbely created a sticker of Day-glo green with the number 51 boldly imprinted on it, Mailer rang my home early in the morning and in a hoarse voice asked me: "What man would vote for a candidate using that faggy green?" Even the numbers upset him, though they were the bold type used on old-fashioned calendars. The 5 had a fancy tail—it was "faggy and liberal." Two days later he was to change his mind completely and confess that the eye-catching sticker really looked good. A week after that he gave permission to order an additional 15,000.

And on it went. Admen would be granted minutes in restaurants or given an audience while he made his way to an elevator, where their work of days would be bluntly and sometimes crudely rejected in front of other people. And doggedly they would go back again to revise what they had done for a campaign that didn't have the money to give it display on television or in a newspaper, even when their work did please the candidate.

One could conjecture that this was Mailer's revenge on the residents of "the Avenue of the Mad," as he once called it, but it was a larger manifestation than that. Mailer was willing to submerge himself in the political role to a point, but he demanded that one keep both eyes open so that the literary figure, the celebrity, also be kept in focus. This duality kept him from learning the ancient political art of dealing with people.

When the press, to his eyes, treated him unfavorably, he didn't respond as a politician but as a writer. They were accused of telling lies about a prizewinning author, America's finest writer, one (after receiving the Pulitzer Prize) "who was honored by their own profession."

The damaging part was not his occasional bad manners but his missed opportunities: the crowds that could have been his, the volunteers who could have been inspired—if he had mastered the little touches instead of relying on the magnetism of his name and reputation. He had come into the toughest playground in America looking for action and partially counting on acceptance because he owned a shiny bat and ball.

With the other marchers came the misbegotten. The disturbed, the lonely, the ones who wanted Mailer to mother their special causes to public attention, and those who just had nowhere else to go. Daily my message box would be filled with handwritten supplications to Mailer to cure the ills of prisons, mental institutions, drunk tanks, and wherever else the lame land. The pleading anxiety of the messages was sad, but they also were foreboding in their intensity. One began to think that political assassination could be the fate of any candidate who turned a deaf ear.

Some of the messages were quasi-religious. One came accompanied by Catholic scapulars for the candidates and the promise of a landslide of rosaries in their behalf. Another read this way:

> To Norman. Study the Torah and Talmud.
> Don't jerk off with politics.
> Talk Israel and don't waste time with your masochistic galut mentality.
>
> Harold Kroudren
>
> P.S. The Blacks will eventually shove you in the oven.

But many a dull day was interrupted by a surprise emerging from our elevator. The old Irishman from the Bronx who "had the goods" on James Scheuer. The "goods" were a property very vague; but after many go-arounds, it was learned that the Irishman was part of the regular machine that Scheuer's machine had defeated. Or the young man from Massachusetts who appeared in a suit, tie, and shirt, looking like an ex-altar boy and seeming perfectly normal as he rendered campaign suggestions—until he informed me that Bobby Kennedy would still be alive if he had listened to him, and that Gene McCarthy would have won the Presidential nomination in Chicago if he had followed his advice to appear on the convention floor wearing a white suit to symbolize his purity.

But I suppose every campaign has someone special on the fringe. Ours had Alexander. He arrived at headquarters during the first week in May—a smallish young man with straight unkempt hair and glasses, his shirt unbuttoned to display a chest on the slight side of Carroll Baker's. If one was looking for something odd, he might venture that such an appearance could fit well in a Bavarian "laBORatory," but stranger sights had got off our elevator. He approached me and inquired if there was anything he could do for the campaign. I suggested petitioning, which he passed off as mundane and asked if there wasn't something "more creative" to be done.

I dismissed him as another celebrity ass-rubber and went about my business, but he pursued to tell me that he was Alexander the Great, Mailer was his Aristotle, and together they would conquer the world with love. He then declared he was going to do something for the campaign that "evoked the spirit of Norman Mailer." He went out and bought a half gallon of cheap wine.

He soon became our oddity in residence. We set aside a special place for him near the back wall at headquarters, where he would sit liquidly "evoking" Mailer. For days he sat writing *Alexander's Histoire* in notebooks, until closing time when I would ask him to help sweep the floor. Since he financed his evocations out of the bucket that held the money from the sale of buttons, I didn't think the request was unreasonable. With the disdain befitting a great warrior who had been deprived of his orderly, he would take the broom and sweep out his own four-by-four-foot tent space, then regally drop the broom on the floor and go back to his wine.

But these were high times, and such incidentals were to be embellished into legend. On Saturday and Sunday, May 3 and 4, the petition drive caught fire. We had more than twenty tables on the streets each day, and we brought in over 6,000 signatures. Dave Block, a young friend of Weinstein's who recently had returned from naval duty in Vietnam, was the largest single producer. He worked every night of the week and all day on weekends. Weinstein spread the rumor that Block's objective was to get the same number of signatures as Lou Gehrig's record for consecutive games, 2,130.

As the numbers started to add up, the volunteers worked harder and longer. It was the old winner's psychosis—for a brief inning we had the establishment beaten, and we wanted to run up the score.

I went to Mailer's house to report our successes, but I soon discovered my newfound elation was to be short-lived. The night before, Mailer had gone to a party given by Tom Quinn for some of his Wall Street friends. Quinn, a broker himself, had just returned from California to reestablish his work in the city. A friend of both Mailer's and mine, Quinn had the kind of background that intrigued the candidate. He was an ex-Marine who during his tour was the East Coast regional boxing champion of the Corps, the ex-manager of welterweight Joe Shaw (a fighter Mailer had a piece of), and currently was regarded as an up and coming light on Wall Street. His burly Irish good looks would be more at home in a squad room than a boardroom, but in a city interested only in "law and order," his mug could be invaluable at the polls—he was the embodiment of our boys in blue, a fact that had not been lost on director Mailer, who had cast him as a cop in his film *Beyond the Law*.

So Mailer delivered his "great idea." He wanted Quinn to run as his controller. I didn't think it was great. We had about 8,000 signatures for the candidates and a little more than a week left to reach our goal of 15,000, and now Mailer wanted me to try to qualify an unknown who was not publicly connected with the ticket in any way. I patiently explained in a voice as mean and ragged as a broken bottle that I didn't think it was possible or, furthermore, even fair, since workers had organized for Mailer and Breslin only, not for a ticket that was going to pull a controller out of a hat.

Quinn arrived at the house suffering from Southern California-itis in blue and white hiphugger pants. (Mailer would ask Quinn to go home and change the pants before meeting Breslin, since

Jimmy "won't take you seriously if you are dressed like that.") The look on my face told Quinn his candidacy wasn't meeting with acclamation. I liked Quinn, but I felt this had nothing to do with friendship. Mailer, in my opinion, was being irresponsible to further complicate matters. Also, Quinn didn't recall the last time he had registered to vote in New York or at what address, so it was conceivable that he was not only ineligible to run for office but even to vote in the election. All these deadly realities managed to bury enthusiasm for Quinn's candidacy before it left the room.

As I was making a grieved Theda Bara exit, Mailer stopped me at the door and said: "How about Torres?" The obscenities scrambled for the opening in my mouth like old ladies for a subway seat. Mailer with malicious glee laughed in my face. He had managed to win the final round.

When I reached headquarters, Tully and Banning had their bitch—namely, Breslin. For the last five days he had been unreachable. He had ignored his entire schedule, incensing the clubs and organizations that backed him. I was to find that he had been hiding out in his agent's office and in Clay Felker's apartment. He saw the campaign as a brief and witty exercise to discredit the regular pols, then an exit before the real campaigning began. Like Buckley, he could make fantastic use of the media, and a press conference or two each week where he could deliver his well-thought-out irreverences was an ideal and civilized way to wage war. But this was different.

There was a headquarters, a staff, Mailer's money, and hundreds of young people to whom he was responsible. He was called upon to make physical appearances in clubs, where he had viewing audiences of only twenty or thirty. All this was far removed from Breslin's original concept of his campaign. The boulevardier, who wished to sit at his table dispensing bon mots as the world sauntered by, was being summoned to get off his seat of knowledge and join the chase.

Besides, there was talk of dark conflict at home. Breslin's casual "walk around" had been turned into a grueling sixteen-hour daily marathon without his permission, and he wanted no part of it. The one certainty in Breslin's world was that he wanted out. On Monday, May 5, the Pulitzer Prize committee opened an exit door in what Breslin thought was the impregnability of his tomb.

Mailer, Newfield, and I met at Maas' apartment on Monday to wait for Bernie Weinraub of the New York *Times*. Weinraub had been assigned to do a political interview with Mailer, but when he arrived, he began asking the candidate questions about his work: Where did he like to write? How many hours a day did he work? and others. He explained that the Pulitzer Prizes were to be announced that day, and the *Times* wanted a story "in case Mailer won." I figured Mailer was in, since I couldn't believe the grande dame of journalism would send its sons on speculative interviews. The question was: Which book? *The Armies of the Night* or *Miami and the Siege of Chicago*?

Headquarters called to say that about 200 kids were sitting on the campus grounds at Queensboro College waiting for Breslin to arrive. No Breslin. He was nowhere to be found. The date had to be covered, since it involved our only constituency, the kids. I, the humble ingenue from Brooklyn, went on. A star was not born.

After this ignominious appearance, I returned to headquarters, where a crowd of newsmen was waiting—Mailer had won the Pulitzer for *The Armies of the Night*. Since he wasn't there, I was called upon once again to play second banana—this time for Canadian television. The interview took place in the back of the room, just feet from where Alexander was composing and drinking. As I was being made up for the camera, he walked over, his eyes glazed. I told him to go back to his seat, he obeyed, and the interview began.

Things went along smoothly until the reporter asked me what Norman Mailer's first act, if he was elected, would be. I mulled it over, trying to think of a magical phrase that would eternally endear us to Manitoba Province, when Alexander bolted from his chair screaming: "I, Alexander the Great, will demand the immediate withdrawal of all troops from Southeast Asia!" I sat there, that pained expression on my face which Dean Rusk reserved for his confrontations with the Senate Foreign Relations Committee, while the camera and microphone beamed in on Alexander. Recovering, I shoved him back into his seat, pushed away the cameraman, and called the sound man an exploiting son of a bitch. We lost Canada.

Apparently, this was to be a day for losses. Breslin's secretary, Karen Burger, a pretty, cheery girl in her twenties who was giving Krakauer and Peebles a hand at the press desk, called me to the phone. It was Breslin. "This is it," he said. "It's a new ballgame. No more fuckin' around."

I asked *what* is *it?* Breslin replied: "I'm calling a press conference. I'm not going to have people make a joke of this, not after what happened today. That prize makes him the biggest man in America. I'm going to quit."

I pleaded with him to hold off until he met later with Mailer at a prearranged dinner date. No, he couldn't be talked out of it —he was through. Finally, he agreed to come to headquarters before he called his press conference, partially because he had to dictate his statement to his secretary. In twenty minutes he arrived, handwritten notes in hand.

Breslin had a tactic he employed whenever he didn't want to discuss something. He would walk about, waving his hands, cutting off all conversation with a short bark, then turn his back and stalk away before you could engage him in argument.

I reached Mailer at a flat on the upper West Side, where he was being interviewed by members of the high school underground press, and put Breslin on the phone while I picked up an extension. Breslin went into his reasons for quitting, but Mailer wasn't buying. Breslin insisted that he was ruining the ticket because he was regarded as a clown. Mailer exploded and told him he was busy "with kids with sharp minds and tough questions," and he wasn't going to worry about Breslin's ego, especially over the phone. They would settle it at dinner. Breslin accepted the hiatus, and we left together for Whyte's restaurant on 57th Street, Breslin carrying his typed swan song in his pocket.

Alexander, who wanted to avenge my insult, followed us into the street. I declined, but he felt his honor had been seriously impaired and only my prone body on Broadway could set things right. Breslin stepped in as referee and cooled the situation when he "loaned" Alexander five dollars.

When we reached Whyte's, Breslin and I made our way to the bar. He ordered a beer and I a soda, though the virtues of the sober life were becoming steadily less impressive. A few minutes later, Alexander entered with his freshly minted five, disdainfully looked at our beer and soda, and moved to the other end of the bar. There, seeking the solace accorded to aggrieved gentlemen, he ordered a double martini.

Breslin tried to convince me his decision was right. Everybody to whom he had talked that day had told him so, he said, including Steve Smith. I argued that he couldn't do this to the campaign and especially to the kids. But he sat firm. I tried my best to be civil but found it hard to go along with Breslin's assertion that his retirement was based strictly on Mailer's winning the Pulitzer Prize.

It was clear after we toured the campuses that Breslin had become disenchanted. The straight politicking at the clubs and organizations held no appeal. Breslin often talks and writes about "friendly vibrations," and apparently he didn't feel them at the clubs. Too, his act didn't go over as well in these settings. Breslin's life is like a Hugo Haas movie—it is starred in, written, produced, directed, and, most important, publicized by Jimmy Breslin. Sadly, the character that projects is one dimensional: the Irish mucker, the barroom *bon vivant* with a "fuck" on his lips and a pint in his hand. Yet this is the same man who wrote so brilliantly and movingly from an intensive care unit in Dallas, a mule-drawn funeral procession in Memphis, and the Siamese hells of Watts and Vietnam. None of this depth ever shows in public.

Some claim the murder of Robert Kennedy drastically wounded him. It's an argument I would not dispute, but I doubt that it had any effect on the public Breslin. His act has been in repertory too long. I have seen minor variations of it all too often in those dark mahogany worlds where Jack Kennedy's picture dominates the top of the bar and planets of shuffleboard pucks endlessly collide while the sexless voices of banshees sugarize "the Troubles."

Breslin allows no one to penetrate the Runyonesque façade of the boisterous belter, the performer who walks the tightrope between the cops and crooks. And you wonder—if his act is that enormous, how huge is the hurt?

Now Mailer had bested him at his own profession, and perhaps he did feel like a deficit to the ticket, for even though he moved well among his own class, he was stepping up in company. As he painfully fiddled with his resignation, my emotions shifted, and I realized we were doing something terrible to James Breslin.

He handed me his statement to read, and I had to laugh in spite of myself. It was composed of hinted truths and downright lies, but for all its chicanery and pandering, it was moving. And once again, you were humbled before political genius when you realized his abdication was worthy of the Duke of Windsor. It went like this:

> Some days ago, at Hunter College, I sat on the stage and listened to Norman Mailer describe the torment of people living in high-rise housing projects. I was depressed, angered and totally moved by his words, and thrilled by the mind producing them. It was clear that I was with a person who will go down as the American genius of the 1960's.
>
> Today, we have a situation which sees the nation starting to recognize the same thing.
>
> There has been some question of credibility surrounding Norman Mailer's candidacy for mayor of the city of New York. I feel this view is not worthy of an answer at this time. The people and publications who have asked this question owe apologies to Mr. Mailer. They also owe him their support. It is clear he is the only mind capable of saving this wounded place we call the city of New York.
>
> I feel Norman Mailer's candidacy is so important at this time that in order to prevent any interference with it; any attempts by others to jab at him with humor or jealousy or fear; it is of the utmost importance that I withdraw today as his running mate.
>
> From this point on, I will organize, research, write and even speak for Norman Mailer. I will work for his campaign 16 hours a day. I will do this with a deep, personal attachment to the campaigner and his campaign.
>
> But I remove myself as candidate for the office of president of the City Council.
>
> Gentlemen, no longer is this a ticket comprised of two writers who can be rumpled and charming and smile-provoking.
>
> You now have Norman Mailer, the American genius of the 1960's, running against Robert Wagner, the dullard of the 1950's.
>
> And you now have Norman Mailer running against Mario Procaccino, the one most preposterous candidate of my time in my city.
>
> I don't think there is any question about what the outcome of the Democratic primary is going to be.
>
> I leave this political race with my head high and the lightest

heart I ever have had. I feel I have performed the utmost service to my city and the people who live and work in it.

I have had a small part in giving this city the only man I know who can save it.

One last thing. If you feel the world is rational and that human beings can be instruments for good, then for God's sake please vote for Norman Mailer.

Newfield and Maas had invited Adam Walinsky, Robert Kennedy's former speechwriter and highly touted *wunderkind*, to have dinner with us at Whyte's. Walinsky, with his wife, Jane, arrived after Maas and Newfield but before Mailer. Breslin tried to recruit their support. It was no dice. There wasn't an ally among us. And since we stood around his seated presence in a semicircle, Breslin was unable to pull off his normal tactic of bellowing and walking away, giving us the back of his back.

When Mailer arrived, he wasn't much solace. He just added another voice to the chorus. The rest of us moved into the dining room, while Mailer and Breslin remained at the bar to hash it out. From the open dining room, one could watch the proceedings. They stood, glasses in hands, mouths and hands moving to score points. For a while it was a contest. Then Mailer put his arm around Breslin's shoulders, and Jimmy's head contritely started to bow. His verbal attack was reduced to bobbing his head as Mailer continued his brotherly cajoling. And when Mailer protectively hugged him and broke into a grin, we realized the prize score for the day was Mailer—2, Breslin—0.

Mailer and a contrite Breslin joined the party at the table in the dining room. I sat next to Mailer at the middle of the table, and Breslin took a seat on his extreme right flank. General von Mailer, never one to miss a tactical error, hissed in my ear: "You stupid son of a bitch. I wanted Breslin in here next to me, not at the end of the table." I looked up to survey the situation and saw the error of my position. Near the end of the table, where Breslin sat, were the stairs. The stairs led to the bar. The bar to a drink. A drink to a reassessment. A reassessment to the phone next to the bar. The phone to the press. The press to a conference. A conference to abdication. A teary Mailer left at the altar. A shambles.

Breslin pushed back his chair, rose, and announced: "Excuse me, I have to go to the men's room." The table turned to ice in apprehension. Breslin stared in innocent bewilderment and left for his destination. Mailer turned to me and cryptically said: "Follow him." Newfield added: "Make sure he doesn't sneak out the front door."

So in my best gumshoe fashion, I hovered off to the side of the door marked GENTLEMEN, blowing smoke rings so casual they yawned. Breslin remained inside for an inordinate amount of time, and I began to fear there was a pay phone in the john. Worse, he still had a carbon of his statement, since I had managed to get only the original from him at the bar. Still no Breslin. Every time the door would open, I would dart back from view. Waiters began to stare at me, and when a middle-aged man exiting from the toilet nervously checked to see if his fly was secure, I realized I'd better rejoin my party. Much to everyone's relief, Breslin came walking in about a minute later.

I wasn't staying for dinner but intended to hang about long enough to get my hands on the other copy of Breslin's statement. Too, I was curious about Walinsky. He had a show-biz aura about him: short, slim, hair flirting with the collar of a broad-black-striped shirt, a wearer of jewelry and rimless glasses, his whole neat ensemble tucked into a pair of black boots.

When he spoke, he used a celery stalk as a pointer; the point established then would be snapped off and deftly devoured by its creator and finally washed down with a drink which he moved to his lips by opening his hand as if it was a fan. He was a dancer —not athletic or graceful, but from the old school where sweat was mistaken for style and motion for movement. His reputation preceded him well, a dynamo. A regular Yankee Doodle Dandy.

He turned to me, saying, "You have the most exciting ticket in town. What you ought to do is get on the air every five minutes with spot ads and shout these guys' names. Drum their names into the public. All day. Every day. Mailer, Breslin." I thought of our budget and politely smiled. It was quite obvious in whose family vineyards Mr. Walinsky had labored.

Breslin started to relax when we were joined by his legendary friend, the bookmaker Fat Thomas. Thomas is a tall, impeccably dressed man with pink, well-scrubbed skin free of blemish and exuding infancy. His gray-white hair gently sits upon the mound of pink as if it were talc. A baby's bottom that takes action.

Fat and Breslin swapped outrageous tales to entertain the table, but their comfort derived from the fact that they had managed to isolate themselves from the others. Breslin had put on his public mantle, and the anxiety of the early evening faded. Not only was he on his own ground, but he had an ally—in fact, an ally he had created. Talk of heist men, lushes, and arsonists continued, and if some stories dealt with sex or in the telling erotic words were used, it made no difference. Jane Walinsky smiled without a sense of threat (one felt Mailer couldn't get away with the same thing); and Breslin, now concrete in his ease, became the adored Irish monument. It was then that I asked for the carbon and extracted a promise from him to fulfill a speaking engagement the following morning. I got both and bid a contented table good night. It had been a day when all of us finally got what we wanted.

The following morning was one to which the candidates had been looking forward. They were to confront the cops at the John Jay College of Criminal Justice, an educational adjunct of the Police Academy. Though Breslin had written columns about the cops, scolding them for their opposition to the civilian review board and the way they handled peace demonstrations, he also had been one of the few writers who had the insight neither to pronounce them pigs nor to plasticize them as saints, but to allow them a working-class dignity. Breslin had another plus going for him. He and the cops were part of the same street fraternity whose cherished password is: "Everyone is on the take."

Mailer would be harder for them to understand. An acknowledged cop fighter and hater, he still was not beyond delivering paeans to the law as Lieutenant Roberts in his novel *The American Dream*, or in his own characterization of an Irish cop in his film *Beyond the Law*. And that was another thing—the Irishness. From Sergius O'Shaugnessy in *The Deer Park* to Roberts to his celluloid mick, Mailer carried on a flirtation with the Celts; and, of course, a large number of New York City's cops are of Irish descent. You sensed that because the Irish gravitated to the cops, the last outpost of legal criminality, they intrigued Mailer. It was a fascination so subterranean, one wondered if the gathered cops would appreciate it.

The college building is on East 20th Street, and the classroom on the fifth floor. An overflow crowd spilled out into the hallway and clustered near each door at the front and rear of the room. The instructor, a young man with a beard, apologized for the conditions and lavishly introduced Breslin as one of the few journalists who has been able to capture the essence of New York from "the Hudson to the East River, with its glitter and excitement and its squalor and pathos." One listened for the strains of "Slaughter on Tenth Avenue" as Breslin took the stage.

He wore his black suit with the sheen, not dull enough for Wall Street, not glistening enough for the Mafia. It fell somewhere between the two worlds, a plainclothesman out on the make. A nice touch.

With his opening statement Breslin let it be known he was familiar with the sound of tin: "I'd like the record to state that

Mailer on the stump in Brooklyn. New York *Times* columnist Tom Wicker is at the left.

Mailer, cropped and clean, on the Staten Island ferry.

Breslin confronts the cops—without a mouthpiece at the John Jay School of Criminal Justice.

The brains behind the throne: Whit Smith (left) and Peter Manso (below).

Two of Mailer's original "hearties:" David Weinstein (above) and Dale Weinstein (below).

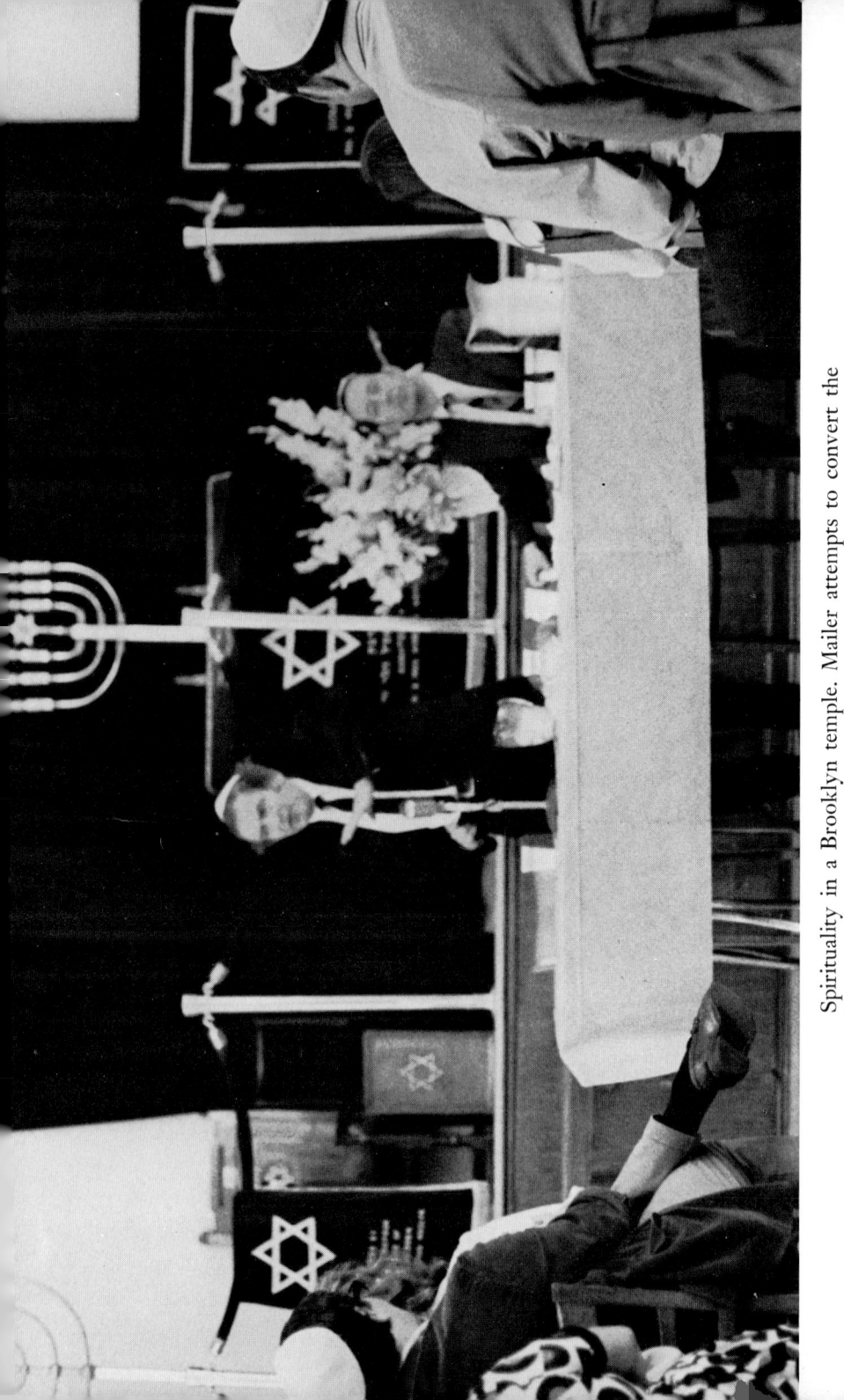

Spirituality in a Brooklyn temple. Mailer attempts to convert the Jews to his cause.

Breslin tries unsuccessfully to woo the women's liberation advocates at Sarah Lawrence. Or, in his jargon, he "ended up going home with the *News and Mirror*."

Jack Newfield (right) puts poison in the pot at the Village Gate fund-raising party. Gerry Pearlman (left) was one of the party's organizers.

Two soul sisters (left and below) add boil and trouble at the Gate.

Big Daddy on the night his "cup runneth over."

Another hard day's night. Beverly Mailer, the candidate, and his campaign manager.

Jack Banning (upper left) during his healthy hairy days.

The accused crops out.

The abused, Sandra Elm, wondered if she'd lost more than a hank of hair.

Once a philosopher, twice a pervert.

Photos by Jack Banning

I'm here without a lawyer." He went on to give the best speech he would deliver during the campaign. It was precisely the kind many of us hoped he would make in white working-class neighborhoods throughout the city. Though it dealt in part with race, it was essentially a class speech that united the white cop (substitute longshoreman, machinist, cabbie—it really doesn't make a difference) with the Black who is getting screwed equally by governmental institutions (Mailer's dull liberal center), indolent congressmen, wasteful bureaucrats, and, indeed, those "who think they're smarter than us plain folk." It was the invasion from underneath we had planned, an assault on the soft underbelly of liberalism. If it was demagogic, its demagoguery had some honest, rough roots, and its delivery was worthy of an urban Huey Long. Gather round now and hearken:

"You know, once I was well liked by the police department, when the man who helped put this building together was commissioner—Mike Murphy. I wrote a column, and he had it reproduced and tacked on the wall in every precinct in the city. And then we got into periods following that where the traffic men would invite me to cross the street and then wave them on and step back and root for a fast Oldsmobile.

"As for my credentials to be here, what can I tell you? I had a cousin who was killed on this job. I grew up in a house with an uncle who was first grade. He was nearly killed on the job, too. You see, there was this girlfriend he had, and he also had a wife who was suspicious. One day he left the house to go to Bergen Street in the car, and his suspicious wife followed him in another car. At Bergen Street, the uncle picked up his girlfriend. That was the extent of his duties at Bergen Street, and they were apparently heading for some sort of outing at the Hotel St. George, when my uncle's wife came up behind them in the car and smashed into them. Her intent was to effect a thing known as homicide. My uncle jumped out and screamed at her: 'What are you, crazy? This broad's my informant.'

"I don't come here as a genius; that's been well established early in my life. I think when the question period comes, I'll be able to learn something from you people, which is good, too, because you're going to get a lot of I-don't-knows from me. But I also have some views on policemen in this city which I'd like to express here. And before I decided to express them, I did look down to see that the chairs were bolted to the floor, and that's going to help. Because the way I see the city, and the way Mr. Mailer sees the city, is that there will be no more New York Police Department as we now know it.

"Our idea is to have this city become a state, have the various sections of this city become cities right inside the state, and let them run their own police. Let's get the wisdom of the neighborhoods, give them the power, and let them run it. I say the plan is far better, from a police viewpoint, than the way we're going, because in my estimation, policemen today are being used. The police get blamed for all the mistakes of all the people who are supposed to be more important and smarter than us. You're asked to go out and take care of, patch up holes made in forty years of history by Congressmen from New York who sat still while federal housing bills were being passed that didn't help us. They sat still while House agricultural committees started a migration—no, forced a migration—from the South into our cities. You're being asked to pay for the actions of union leaders who didn't do a thing for ghetto areas of this city and have kept people jobless. And when they're jobless, they look to do things.

"You're being asked to pay for a Board of Education which sat at 110 Livingston Street and kept everybody in the city illiterate in the areas you worry about most. And you're being asked to pay for the mistakes of white politicians who walked around and never even knew one Black person and made the decisions which affected their lives and caused an awful lot of the rancidness that's now in everyone's mouth over this situation. Now they created the problems. Now they turn to you, the policemen of the city of New York, and say: 'You go out and handle them.' In my estimation, it's a disgrace. As usual it comes down to us—give it to the fellow on the bottom. Let him handle the problem.

"They send fellows into Harlem and Bedford Stuyvesant or Brownsville or East New York—white policemen. I think it's insanity. It's an expression of enormous ignorance. Those days are gone when white people can rule the Black neighborhoods. I think the days also should be gone that we should ask a white person to go in there. A fellow who is a cop with a wife and three children home, and he comes into the city eight hours a day, and you send him into an area where he's disliked, despised, it produces a volatile situation. I don't think that makes any sense at all. I think we're asking too much of our fellows.

"Now this city is in trouble, and the main thing we need is respect for law and its officers. But Black people never again will respect law under the present conditions. They just won't respect this law, and they're not going to respect the people who are instruments of it. That's been proven. Just walk around any block. I mean you walk down Sumner Avenue in Brooklyn, you hear what they say behind your backs. This is insanity if you let it go on. And out of it you get the fear, and you get the quick reactions which shouldn't be there.

"What we feel the problem is is that people in these neighborhoods, in all neighborhoods, have got to run their own schools and their own police. You've got Boys' High School in Bedford Stuyvesant. It's four blocks from the Seventy-nine. I think Boys' High would make an excellent feeder for the Seventy-ninth Precinct. I don't think Massapequa, Long Island, is a good feeder for the Seventy-ninth Precinct. I think if you had police cadet training starting in high school, instead of these gym classes they have, they'd be able to find their own source of policemen for those areas, and they could run their own police departments. Certainly, I think the neighborhood would be in a lot better shape law-wise than it is now.

"Let *me* tell you what you're up against in figures. The one thing I'll tell you, they tell you to 'go in there and take care of this matter; you're ours, we love you.' There are candidates who come around with 'God bless you, boys, you're the line between us and doom.' But *they* don't tell you what you're up against in figures.

"We'll take one high school in this city. Benjamin Franklin High School. Next month one thousand grade school transcripts are going to be received there from kids who are supposed to come to school in September. In September only seven hundred of these kids show up. Right away, you got three hundred kids out running on the streets. I don't have to tell you what that means. Over a four-year period, after four years, of these seven hundred who start in Benjamin Franklin, seventy-five of them wind up with academic diplomas; three hundred graduate—they're given some certificate of attendance. A certificate of attendance at Benjamin Franklin High School normally entitles a kid to push junk—it has no meaning whatsoever. That means seventy-five out of an original list of a thousand are at the end of four years, hopefully, citizens. This leaves nine hundred and twenty-five kids running around streets without an education, without any hope, with a very low reading level, some don't speak English, and they wind up as your problem. But you're told to go out there and handle it, and the Board of Education is sitting there every day—creating criminals for you. I think we have to decentralize the situation. Let these neighborhoods run their own schools. They can do far better than we've done. You mean to tell me that in East Harlem, on 115th Street and

Pleasant Avenue, which is where Benjamin Franklin High School is, they can do any worse than graduate seventy-five out of a thousand? I don't see how that can be done.

"The whole thing we feel is that the situation in this city has to be ventilated. We talk about urban problems in the past. The urban problem now is a color problem—it starts in this city. We think the only way that this can be handled is to send everybody to his own room, and we'll talk in the morning. But we've got an awfully long night to go through first. Let's ventilate, let's separate, let's have people in control of their own education. Make this city a state, and later on somewhere along the line we can start to mingle. I think the people are much better at controlling their own destiny.

"With that, I think I'm going to step down, except for one thing—you had a class about bookmaking in here first. I could bring in a guest lecturer for that anytime you want."

Mailer, who was introduced as "America's visionary in residence," was next. Following the line of a three-time loser who had nothing left to lose, he spilled everything. His shady past was bared to one and all:

"Well, these are strange times, aren't they? Now, I know most of you feel that to that splendid eulogy one more term could be added, which is 'cop-hater.' I've had that reputation for years. Whenever it began to die, *Time* magazine would revive it. They would say: 'Cop-hater Norman Mailer said today that the grass in Prospect Park was not as green as it used to be.' And, in fact, there were years of my life when I was a cop-hater. There were years when I hated some of you guys so much it wasn't funny. As recently as three years ago, when José Torres was fighting Wayne Thornton at Shea Stadium, I was trying to get to his dressing room—I will confess I had had about eight drinks before I started—and I was intercepted by a cop in the alley under the stands. I'm very proud of that day, because it was the last time I ever went ape. I'm not really a very strong fellow, but that day I was so determined to get to José Torres' dressing room that ten cops were holding me, and we were moving like a wave, back and forth. It was the only time in my life I've ever been strong enough to be on even terms with ten cops. Let me tell you, since I'm as yellow as any good cop, no punches were thrown by anyone. Just a tremendous number of names went back and forth, mostly from me. New York's finest were finer that day than your humble visionary.

"Nonetheless, I have, and I admit this frankly, been obsessed as a novelist for years with the character of cops, because it seems to me that the one thing nobody ever gives a cop credit for is that he's a very complicated guy. And a good cop is a fantastically complicated guy. In fact, I've talked to little left-wing groups, students, student undergrounds, revolutionaries, Black Panthers, and I've argued with them about one thing. I've said to them that you've got to recognize that a good cop is a work of art, and that when you call cops pigs you're always hurting the best cops on the force, because you are polarizing them down to the level of the worst cops on the force."

A large part of what he said worked. With their parochial belief that confession is good for the soul (and for their business), the cops were impressed by Mailer's contrition. The line "I'm as yellow as any good cop," of course, gave their collective conscience pause, but they let it pass, realizing that in every squeal, there's some hustle. He went on to talk about his film on cops, noting that it was superior to anything that Hollywood had fashioned. Then he offered his *pièce de résistance*: the reason why New York City should become the fifty-first state, and how the cops would benefit. It was a slice of philosophy that aptly could be called Keystone, since it chased everyone else's notion of law and order all over the lot and left his audience panting, their brains out of breath from the dizzy go-around.

"Everybody in this city has more ideas than they can practically keep in their heads. And there's no place for these ideas to go, because the entire legislative thicket of this city, of this city charter, impedes every honest man, or in fact every dishonest man, from making any kind of quick or interesting move. So neither the cops nor the crooks have a chance to get any better. And my idea, parenthetically, is that a good society doesn't depend upon having a great police force or having a great criminal element in society, which certain revolutionaries would believe, you guys would say, but rather that a good society depends upon the cops *and* the crooks getting better. Think about it. It's an unusual notion, but the idea behind it is if they both get better, everybody is doing more every day, which means you've got a richer society in terms of the real life that people are living."

It all went too easily. The questions that followed were polite and informed and the responses well received. Was it possible that the cops could be converted in a day? When we were about to leave, we got our answer. About twenty uniformed policemen began to file into the room, and one of them, spotting Breslin, shouted: "Hey, Jimmy, aren't you going to stay and talk to us? The real cops? These guys never get out on a beat; they all work inside. They're fuckin' liberals."

Since classes weren't mandatory at the college, our audience wasn't representative of the force. Those who attended classes were more progressive in their approach to police work (or "fuckin' liberals," if you walked that philosophical beat). Indeed, many of the Academy students were not yet on the force at all. In short, the degree we had just received was a long way from the third.

The cops piled into the vacated seats, shouting to the candidates to stay. Neither could resist the challenge, and the cops began to grill. "If you and Breslin go ape on the same evening," one asked Mailer, "who will run the city?" Mailer answered that it was unlikely that would happen on the same night, but a provision to cover such an eventuality could be put into the city-state constitution.

Another shouted, "Come on, Jimmy, give us some bullshit about what you're going to do for us." Breslin first mocked Scheuer's position favoring the use of voluntary policemen: "All those guys would sit in cop cars and ask, 'Please let me blow the siren.'" (When this comment appeared in print in the *Times* the next day, the chief of the auxiliary police force sent me a letter, followed by a phone call, demanding a formal retraction from Breslin—which he never received.) Then he added, "And I won't give you that other bullshit of 'God bless you, boys, we need you tonight' that those other clowns give you."

That one hurt, and another cop jumped in: "What about all those fuckin' long-haired punks, Jimmy?" Breslin slipped it to him with a smile: "You'd better be careful. Those kids got a lot to say. And besides, have you checked your own kids' hair lately?"

It was a wild shot, but Breslin caught some piece of home. The cop exploded: "Fuck all those kids. In my opinion they have nothing to say. Nobody under eighteen has anything to say. And I have my doubts about you with your long, curly hair." The cop's ultimate trump card—the queen—which he played with abandon like all his brothers, wildly flinging it out to punish anyone who questioned any part of his canon. (How many delicious interpretations that word offers.)

But the cop had played it too soon, too rashly. Showing real gutter style, Breslin let him have it from the bottom of the deck: "I wouldn't walk into a piss house with you alone either, baby."

So it went, the cymbals of their life-styles banging off each other, interrupted by an occasional chanting chorus of "We want Mario, we want Mario." Mailer stood at the bottom of the stage swapping philosophy with about six cops. Breslin, his right leg drawn over his left like a crossbow, sat on the edge of the stage looking curiously pink and young, as he gleefully rocked back and forth while the bulk of the audience surrounded and interrogated him. The sages of the sewer's-eye view of the city hounded him, but it was no match. He repelled them with wit, invective, and sheer long-windedness. Today, the prize was his. The gutter child, our savior of the streets, had finally found his temple.

It was May 7, and the petitions had to be delivered to the Board of Elections by May 13. Our count now was about 8,700, and I knew we were home. But we still had five days to add a cushion, so the staff and I poor-mouthed our position to keep everyone hustling. This tactic proved unnecessary, since the town was beginning to discover Mailer and Breslin, and the kids could feel it. Our buttons—NO MORE BULLSHIT—MAILER & BRESLIN and VOTE THE RASCALS IN—began to sell out as quickly as an order came in.

The press started to play us up—not always in the fashion we wished, but it was coverage. So far, it had been a dull campaign, sagging under the weight of Wagner's ennui, Procaccino's law-and-order clichés, Badillo's predictable decency, and Scheuer's money. A dull campaign in a sad city with a grimace of despair carved into its face.

Mailer and Breslin managed, for a short season, to turn that grimace into a grin. A grin that the political naïveté in the campaign would interpret as a forthcoming shower of votes. The lesson they missed is that New Yorkers are like all parents: even though the daughter they have to bestow is a slattern, the most unkempt bitch in the Western world, she is all they have and is not to be squandered on charmers, carousers, and midnight philosophers, but should be neatly handed over to the nine-to-five opposition.

The problem was that Mailer and Breslin were trying to woo property—dubious turf, no doubt, but all the city residents had. The candidates were loved, but not trusted. If it had been possible to give them else, most New Yorkers would have complied. One could almost hear in the air the New York plaint of a Jewish mother: "Leave my daughter alone. Go screw around with Des Moines."

It was with high spirits that we prepared for a huge fund-raising party to be held that evening at the Village Gate, a Greenwich Village club. Our money problems had never improved. Mailer still was putting in more of his money than any of us wanted. (He had just signed over his $1,000 Pulitzer Prize check to the campaign.) And it seemed the New York *Times* had taken care of any substantial outside contributions when they broke a story reporting that Mailer would receive $1,000,000 for covering the moon shot for *Life* magazine in July. The quoted sum was totally out of proportion, perhaps a *Times* error or Mailer's agent blowing his own horn with a Gabriel-like wind. Whatever the source, it crippled us financially for the rest of the campaign. But if the *Times* was going to print such an outrageous figure, they also could have added that if Mailer won the primary, he would not have covered the event but remained in New York to wage his fight for the mayoralty. For if a man has trouble establishing the seriousness of his intentions, what better proof of it than to forfeit $1,000,000, an act that in this society would cause him to be committed or granted the solemnity of the Sphinx.

There had been rumors that our petitions would be challenged by both Badillo and Scheuer. In an effort to head this off, Tully had called aides in both camps, whom he knew, and invited them "downtown for drinks at the Gate." Our strategy was that he and I would try to convince the respective aides that Mailer and Breslin really were the Rover Boys out for a lark, and "if your candidates challenged *them,* they will look absurd." Conviviality failing, we would use pressure. If they insisted on challenges, we would discredit them in the liberal community as machine politicians and personally slander them among the young volunteers. The enemy accepted the invitations, and the evening was set.

I wanted the volunteers to make the most of their first full evening off, so I decided to clean up and close the headquarters myself. Also, for most of them, it would be their first chance to meet Mailer and Breslin, and I wanted them to get good tables up front.

By 11 P.M. the place was empty, except for Alexander, who was sitting in the rear with a half gallon of wine. He asked me to share a cab downtown, but I refused, saying I was waiting for my wife. The real reason was that I planned to take 9,000 signed petitions downtown to lock in Art D'Lugoff's safe. Strange fires and thefts have been known to take place in campaign headquarters near the end of petition drives, and I was taking no chances. Also, I didn't fancy Alexander's sloshing his wine on our entry fee all the way to the Village. I'd be damned if we were going to be disqualified for muscatel-scented petitions.

The inducement of cab fare coaxed Alexander to go without me, but with his wine. When my wife arrived, we went out onto a rainy Broadway, I with the petitions in a box under my arm, shielding them from the rain with newspapers, until a cab stopped. Like a doting father, I thanked the cabbie as I placed my precious bundle on the seat first while the rain fell on us.

My fear of drawing a meager crowd was quelled when the cab pulled up outside the Gate. The sidewalks were jammed with a collection of kids, freaks, the curious straight people, and that pathetic group of Villagers who have never been weaned from the tit of fashion. But they all held their hot five-dollar bills in their hands, so with the mentality of a hooker, I decided to look at the ceiling and fake enthusiasm.

I put the petitions in the office safe and headed for the door, where Judy Freed was taking tickets. She is a middle-aged woman who is attractive in that peculiar lacquered New York sort of way. She had had experience sticking up the go-go set in the city for every cause imaginable, and tonight she was dead on target. They were clawing to get inside the doors.

Inside, the Gate was pulsating with rock 'n' roll and throbbing lights that resembled corpuscles on a rampage. It was probably because of the antiquated fondness I have for stand-up saloons, but nonetheless I felt like Nathanael West's Balso Snell, meandering around inside someone's intestines. The New York Rock and Roll Ensemble had donated its services for the rally, and the musicians, frocked in Edwardian splendor, were creating an electric storm on stage. A solid bar of cobalt from movie and television lights and crocheted flashbulbs pointed out Mailer's table.

The setup didn't please me. The volunteers who had performed all the dog work for the last three weeks had been shuffled off to tables on the fringes without anything to drink, while at Mailer's booze-laden table sat Farber, whose contribution to the campaign was Cinderella-like in that he would attend all the balls till midnight, and Bill Walker, an ex-welterweight from the South who also was a Provincetown friend of Mailer's and made his living from time to time as a bouncer in Village bars. I had met Walker on one or two occasions before, and he seemed pleasant enough and totally devoted to Mailer; but the fact of the matter was that he had not been active in the campaign up to this point. Mailer should have had the political judgment to be among his workers.

Hovering nearby, of course, was Parmentel, Mailer's link to the right wing, making his first appearance since the initial party at Mailer's home. Parmentel, William F. Buckley, and the state chairman of the Conservative Party, Kieran O'Doherty, constitute that new breed of the white proletariat who speak and write in an overdressed, drag ball style, forever flashing rhinestones of reference to celebrities, events, and places—perhaps in an attempt to impress their leftist audience that they hadn't attended the same vocational schools as the people they were supposed to represent.

The order of the evening called for Newfield to speak first and introduce Breslin. I would follow Jimmy to make a pitch for more money (to be collected by ten volunteers stationed around the hall, symbolically carrying breadbaskets supplied by D'Lugoff), and Mailer would provide the finale.

As soon as Newfield began speaking, the evening went sour. Perhaps it was the cannibalistic quality of the crowd, or that we were on our own turf, or that Newfield—after working under the tight rein of the Kennedys—felt this was a campaign in which he could exhibit his radicalism or vent his spleen. Whatever the cause, he lost control and set an undisciplined, obscene tone for the evening. He asked members of the audience to come to our headquarters in the morning to form "a guerrilla graffiti squad." They would be supplied with chalk, so they could scrawl our campaign slogan, "No More Bullshit," all over the city. The slogan was innocuous enough, but this was not my idea of how to employ workers. Then he stepped over the line of taste. Referring to a newspaperwoman by name, who we felt was giving the campaign an unfair press, he said that we also were running on another slogan we wanted chalked all over town, that the lady in question was "a lousy lay." Breslin buried his head in his hands, and I winced. Newfield might have been running on that slogan, but it was news to me that Breslin and Mailer were.

Breslin followed with some beery conviviality about how he

had thought running was going to be a wonderful lark until Mailer had shown up "in that goddamn blue suit of his and his hair slicked down with grease." It was a good performance, Breslin portraying himself as a beery Pagliacci suddenly trapped in circumstances beyond his control. As he was drawing to a close, I asked Mailer to wait in the back of the hall to avoid embarrassment when I made my pitch for money. He was drinking and had a pleasant high on, but he was far from drunk and good-naturedly complied.

I gave a short recitation of my woes as campaign manager, making a few lame jokes about how I might be the first manager to die from a liver ailment rather than a heart attack. The reception was as limp as the delivery, but it was no great blow to my vanity, since I was fully aware that I possessed a public speaking style that could dampen the enthusiasm of Germans. So I did what I was supposed to do and called for the volunteers to pass the baskets.

A young Black girl near the stage, pathetically drunk, weaved her way onto it. Something went very dead in my stomach. She walked toward me and the microphones, whining, "I want to say something." At first, there were shouts of encouragement from the audience, perhaps in anticipation of the delicious sting of a black whip on the backside of their minds. Honky dorey. But no such luck. The girl was helpless. She asked how many Black people were there, because she needed their help to get back her job at a hospital that had dismissed her. The audience was embarrassed now, and disappointed. Their hope of having found a scalding militant to torment Mailer's whiteness disappeared. Instead, a gelatinous disease oozed through the crowd.

How to get her off? If she had been white, it would have been easy; but how, in the year of the revolution, do you manhandle a Black woman? Suddenly, a white sister appeared at the base of the stage, spicing the cauldron with double trouble. Beating on its floor with a drumstick, she chanted: "Tell 'em, Joanie, don't let 'em stop you. Tell 'em, Joanie, honey." They crooned, back and forth, a harlequin plague infecting everyone in the room.

As I was trying to usher her off, Mailer, looking very different from minutes ago, mounted the stage. He knew that his evening had been destroyed, and only an act of murder could exorcise the house of devils. He was prepared to commit it. He addressed himself to the girl and the audience at the same time:

"Now look, let me talk, because it's my evening, and you know it. Hey, look, I listened to you a long time, and I'll tell you why I listened to you. I'll tell you why there are no Black people here tonight. It's a simple reason. It's because Adam Clayton Powell has not decided whether he's going to declare yet or not, and the Black people know they would be foolish to declare for a maverick candidate until Adam Clayton Powell has made up his mind. It's as simple as that."

While he was speaking, someone managed to get her off the stage. Mailer then performed a Stanislavskian miracle—he grew fat and sweaty before our eyes! He also launched into his much-heralded Southern accent. It was a performance to humble Rod Steiger's in *In the Heat of the Night*. Like Melville, Mailer strongly suspects that in the end evil will dominate. Before him was the collective, mushy innocence of liberalism: pampered little Billy Budds, a host of angelic fags. And what could be more evil to these towheads than the specter of the sweaty, rhino-fatted, thumbs-in-belt, small-town Southern sheriff? Mailer proceeded to unleash everything but the dogs on them.

The speech that follows is complete, since its delivery had profound effects on both Mailer and the campaign, and also to preserve it for posterity. Because if my notion about man is right, the numbers of people who in years to come will have "personally" heard the speech will grow in legions equal to those who stood in Dublin's General Post Office in 1916 or who sat in the Polo Grounds in 1951 when Bobby Thompson brought the Miracle of Coogan's Bluff full circle. It is a phenomenon which leads one to believe that man is an historic snob and a goddamn liar, or that the walls of these buildings have the same elasticity as a camp follower's and the easy accessibility as well.

"All right, now look, let me have your attention. Really. Let me try something. Can you hear me without the mike? ["No," they yelled.] All right now, let's get into a couple of very simple small bags, which is, one, we're in the Village Gate, which has the worst psychedelic acoustics in the whole world. The acoustics in this place are hooked [From the audience a heckler shouted, "Play 'Melancholy Baby,' Norman." "Fuck you," Mailer replied and continued], are hooked out of Art D'Lugoff's beard. And I love Art, 'cause he is an ogre just like me, and Art decided a long time ago that he was expendable, but he said to the whole world and New York, 'To hell with you, shove it up your screw. I am here. I am running the Village Gate. You cannot stop me unless you come in here and wipe me out.' And they never came in, and Art created a neighborhood. Now the reason I hate talking into this mike—the reason I hate talking into this mike is because it sets up a hypnotic trance which is full of the weaker bullshit in our continuing relationship. [At this point cameramen started crowding him for close-ups, and Mailer, sensing a threat, began to back off, flailing his arms and saying in a cornered voice, "Now get away from me, everybody."]

"Now, look, look, look. Let's be sensible for a while. You're just nothing but a bunch of spoiled pigs. And there ain't a cop in the house. And yesterday I went up to the Police Academy and talked, not to the cops first, but to the students at the John Jay Criminal Justice Academy or whatever it is called. [Reporters, now aware that they had a chance to record a political disaster of *Titanic* proportion, closed in again. Intimidated,

Mailer retreated again. "*Please* get away from me and stop all this dull bullshit. I'm on to it—I'm on to it. Don't interrupt me when I'm talking. I'll be interrupted soon enough. Now next, yeah, next ... look ..." A campaign worker beseeched from the audience, "Norman, talk about the fifty-first state, you're among friends." Mailer thought differently. "Hey, I'll tell you something. Shut up. You're not my friend if you interrupt me when I'm talking, 'cause it just breaks into the mood in my mind. So fuck you. Boo!"]

"All right. I said you're all a bunch of spoiled pigs. You're more spoiled than the cops. I'll tell you that. I'll tell you that. You've been sittin' around, jerkin' off, havin' your jokes for twenty-two years. Yeah. And more than that—more than that. You all want to work for us, you get in there and you do discipline, and you do your devotion. You get in there, and you do some dull work. Don't come in there and help us, because 'we're gonna give Norm a little help.' Fuck you. You help us or don't come near us. I'll tell you why. 'Cause we can win this thing. We can win it if we're very good. We can win it with all of you angels and devils. But we can't win it—we can't win it, if you come in here with your dull little vanities.

"The cops I talked to yesterday were a more impressive group of people than all of you. I'll tell you that. Now is there anybody here who is not familiar with our program by now? No one? All right, then this I say to you. This I say to you. You are all going to go through a tremendous hour of horror, panic, and vomit if you start to work seriously for us, because you know I'm not the only nearsighted crazy man in America, and some of you could get hit. Get it straight. If you're gonna come in and work for us, then work, but leave your ego at the door.

"If you think I'm in this for fun, then I feel sorry for you, 'cause I might have to pass on you after I have gone through. Got it? Got it? All right. Then fuck you. Got it? If you're gonna help me, then help me. But I don't want any of those dull mother tired ego trips. Work.

"Now, to prove to you how good this mayoralty is gonna be—I did not quit while I was ahead. I am about to reinvest my winnings and see if I can capture some of the more delicate spirits in the house. The point to what we're up to is that we are either running in fun or not. Since the neighborhood assembled has only one thing in common, which is they have a ticklish little liver and anus on the notion of who is putting who on. Ha. Ha. They think that we are running in fun. Some of our own people put out campaign buttons like 'Mailer-Breslin, Seriously?' Let me point out to you one quick little notion. Anyone who is runnin' in fun in the mayoralty election in New York deserves to run in fun. ["Profound," someone yelled from the back.]

"Now, I wanna finish with a small story which you can shove down your throats. Years ago, I went out with the distinguished novelist Mr. Ralph Ellison to Iowa for a schlock magazine called *Esquire* run by a martinet and tyrant named Harold Hayes, who wouldn't know a good piece of writing until the Pulitzer Prize kicks him in the back of the ear. One of my dearest friends. And we went out there. A little fellow named Mark Harris—he's a little Jewish fellow with a big cigar which he blew in everyone's face, he's a tiny version of Groucho Marx. And Dwight MacDonald, looking like he was gonna die of asthma and apoplexy twenty-two years ago, and Ellison and myself. And we went out there to Iowa, and we said—this is back in 1959—over and over again that 'the country is in a terrible time. It is full of the worst disease. You don't begin to know how bad this country has become. You people in Iowa have to recognize this is a marvelous state, Iowa, but it really doesn't begin to know how awful things are outside.' And we got this marvelous applause, and we kept saying that people in Iowa—we didn't know the word 'turned on'—we kept saying people in Iowa are marvelous, until we found out they all were graduate students from Michigan and, ah, places like, ah, Philadelphia. So when it was over, like a high school team that fought a very good game and finally lost in the last quarter, I turned to Ellison in the dressing room—we were having some drinks with some marvelous-looking Republican women—and I said, 'Ralph, what the hell do we do it for? Why do we work so hard?' And he said, 'Well, we're expendable.' So get that into your head.

"There's a very simple little notion going on which is we're all going to run, and we're gonna do our best, and we'll go on for eighty-two years or more. But the notion to get through your heads is to get over your silly little ego tired trips. If you have a lot of money and that's the way that you turn on to workin' for us, then thank you very much. We can use that money if you give it to us, and you can give it to us any way you want—publicly, privately, quietly, at large or small. If you have other ways of working for us, work for us.

"What we really want is to get out into the neighborhoods. I want to go out and talk in every neighborhood before I'm done. I'll talk in the sweetest neighborhoods and the worst neighborhoods. But I'm running on the notion that New York can't begin to become the incredibly absolute and magnificent city that it is until there is power to the neighborhoods. Two weeks ago at the end of a long evening of campaigning, speaking at a marvelous—to me—Irish club in Park Slope, overcome with happiness, I said, 'I am running on everything from Black Power to Irish self-righteousness,' and the good Irishmen in that place laughed and applauded, and I thought I had a victory until I read in the *Village Voice* that the smell of political death was upon us. I know what the fellow was up to. He was saying—get out of this campaign. You're just a little Jewish fellow from Brooklyn, and you don't know what's up. Well, let me tell you something. I know what's up because the greatest Jewish paper in New York, the despicable New York *Post*, won't print a word of what we're up to. And let me tell you what that means. Let me tell you this—I am proud of my people. Very few people understand the Jews, but I do, 'cause I'm one of them. [A few of the others started to clap, but tonight Mailer was a majority of one—NO OTHER JEWS NEED APPLY. He censured them with "Fuck you, let me talk."]

"The Jews are an incredible people at their best. At their worst they are swine. Like every WASP I ever met at their worst. They are awful. All people are awful at their worst. Some are worse than others. But the Jews are sensational at their best, which is rare enough, given Miami and a fur coat. Don't laugh, because you don't know what you're laughing at. Okay, don't laugh. Think about it. Whenever a people loses its highest race, there's nothing funnier going on in the world.

"What we're running on is this: that it has come to the point where this town, that many of us grew up in, the greatest city in the history of the world conceivably, is now some sort of paralytic victim in an orphan asylum or the governmental syndrome. And if this city is not saved by a vigorous activity by everybody within it, and I'm not just talking in my cups.... But as the people of New York turn on and become fantastic, which we all are, because I've met more interesting people in New York, per capita, than anywhere else in the world. [Here, the sophisticated natives became sentimental and applauded themselves, but there was room only for one in the love bed tonight, and Mailer rejected the pleasure of their company. "Come on," he said, "let's not spend any time on applause."] Let's get to the point. The point is simple. Unless this city turns on and becomes fantastic, it'll become the first victim of the technological society—you know what that means? That means that the smog, the dull dead air of oppression, will be upon us first, and we will destroy each other first, because we all have too much within us to be able to bear the unendurable dullness of our days in New York when we all know we're capable of so much more. So this I say to you. If we don't save our city, our city will become that little ward. . . . There'll be a fifty-mile bypass around us, and they'll say, 'We understand there are three divisions of Marines in there to keep the populace down.' [The audience applauded the apocalyptic vision, but the massa was callin' in the hounds now: "No, keep quiet. Let me finish, 'cause I'm talkin' very hard. Look, don't come here to be entertained."]

"We're into somethin' that's deep. Don't kid yourself on this. We're runnin' on the notion of power to the neighborhoods. What we're saying is very simple. [A critic down front agreed, "You bet!" But only one horn would blow this midnight. "Shut up and fuck you. Let *me* talk," Mailer declared.] We're here on something very simple, which is that nobody knows any longer which idea has more validity than another, because there's no ground, no content, there's no situation for an idea. We're running on one notion. Let the left and the right have their neighborhoods. Let them each see what kind of society they can create and then decide on the basis of a thousand contests and one hundred bloody encounters, that too, which particular neighborhood, or style, or conception of life is more interesting than another. Let people at least be ready to begin to put their notion of existence behind themselves, in front of themselves, within themselves. Let them begin to work for something they believe in. Nobody in this city can begin to work for anything they believe in, 'cause it just isn't there, it just doesn't exist. This city is controlled from without. That's why everybody is going crazy in this city—because they have no objective correlative, which I remind you literary people is a remark first coined in twentieth-century cultural history by T. S. Eliot, of all people. Well, let me tell you this. There is no objective correlative in this city, but we say power to the neighborhoods would give an objective correlative that would give a notion of where everybody is.

"We are running on one profound notion. Free Huey Newton —end fluoridation. We're running on another profound notion— compulsory free love in those neighborhoods which vote for it, compulsory church attendance on Sunday for those neighborhoods who vote for that.

"What we are running on is one basic simple notion, which is that till people see where their ideas lead, they know nothing. And that, my fine friends, is why I am running. I want to see where my ideas lead. Thank you very much."

I was awestruck when he finished and looked around to see if it was only me. Walker had drunkenly cheered him on from the table, but Breslin's broad back could be spotted making for the exit. Mailer, sporting a satisfied grin, like he was Jack Kennedy after winning over the ministers in Houston, dismounted the stage. Indeed, he walked up to me and gave me a cheery wink and punch as though we had pulled it off together. My senses were out of control. I had no barometer of what had *really* taken place. It was then that Tom Quinn walked up to Mailer. Solid Quinn, the short-cropped financier, the gung-ho Marine who was given to singing "The Teddy Bears' Picnic" when he was in his cups. Surely, Quinn would put it all in perspective. He faced Mailer squarely, a boozy tear in his eye, and said: "Norman, you son of a bitch, I love you." And with a teddy-bear hug: "You remind me of my father!"

I headed for a door to get some air, when I heard someone remark: "I like his idea of neighborhood control, but I wonder if he would let me leave mine to visit my mother on Sundays." Cummings was standing near the rear door in shock. As I approached, his eyes widened as if he was coming to his senses, but I was to realize it was only a vibration of a larger blast to come. I heard it in all its acoustical magnificence: "HE WAS RIGHT. YOU ARE ALL PIGS. DO YOU HEAR? THIS IS ALEXANDER THE GREAT SPEAKING." I turned to see Alexander on stage beating on his bare chest, Wally Cox playing King Kong. "YOU SHALL MARCH UNDER US TOGETHER," he roared.

Workers were running toward the stage to seize him, and Mailer was screaming at him to get down. Betrayed by his mentor, he turned and shouted to Mailer: "CHICKENSHIT!" Mailer was heading toward the stage when Krakauer, the Jewish Florence Nightingale, sang out across the room: "Nobody hit him. He'll kill himself." As quickly as it started, it was over. Alexander was ushered to the door, and the rest of the audience calmly gathered their belongings, as if they had just spent another evening off-Broadway. I stood there, crushed, when a boyhood friend, Ace Gillen, approached me and offered solace. "Don't worry about it," he said. "You don't think anyone believed this evening was for *real?* For Christ's sake, I just heard D'Lugoff wants to book the whole fuckin' act for three months!"

The next day everything was coming apart at the seams. The kids walked around headquarters dazed, looking like they had been slapped in the face. Petitioners wanted to quit. Sosler, who wanted Mailer to take a day out of his schedule and fly to Syracuse University for a speaking date with a guarantee of $1,500 and the possibility of a $3,000 fee, had quit when Mailer flatly refused to go and abused him in the bargain before he abused everyone else at the Gate. That left me without a finance chairman.

The gentlemen from the ad firm of Kurtz and Kambanis called early to assure us that they had *never* been connected with the campaign, concluding, I presumed, that life was happier with Rocky. Breslin had called Newfield at 4 A.M. and drunkenly croaked: "Why didn't you tell me I was running with Ezra Pound?" And at the last word, he was seeking sanctuary in a monastery or a saloon. I began checking the morning newspapers for stories captioned "Tiger at the Gate."

Mailer was out on a tour of Harlem, visiting various projects and community workshops with Banning and Sid Zion, who was doing a story for the *Times*. Better, I thought, that he was covering us today, rather than the night before. So far, nothing was in the papers. Breslin called, looking for news. I told him everything so far was good. He was furious and ready again to quit. I tried to talk him out of it, using once more the argument that he would crush the kids about whom he cared so much. He exploded, and I got the first hint that perhaps Breslin didn't enjoy playing second banana at all: "Why didn't that other son of a bitch worry about the kids last night? He embarrassed me, too. Who does he think he's kidding? I'm the big man in this town. I'll run his ass off the boards!" He said he'd call me later when the afternoon *Post* came up.

We had the good fortune that a "family" newspaper would have trouble reporting the event. There was a story in the *Post*, but it was harmless; in fact, it might have helped us. Mailer was quoted as saying he didn't want ego trippers but hard workers for his campaign, a fine serious note about our intentions. When Breslin called, I read him the story and he calmed down. I decided to see Mailer in the morning to have it out with him. Something had to be done to square it with the kids. Besides, there were five valuable days left for petitioning, and with shell-shocked troops they would be wasted. As far as the press was concerned, it looked like we were home free.

Before I finished breakfast the following morning, I realized I'd been wrong. I was leafing through the *Times*, looking for Zion's Harlem story, when I found his byline on an article captioned "Mailer Plays a Nightclub Date in Bid for Mayoral Nomination." It was all there: Mailer, whiskey glass in hand, Southern accent, four-letter expletives, the shouts of "Play

'Melancholy Baby,' Norman," and Breslin running for the back door. Zion had been at the Gate in a social capacity, but when the paper heard of the performance and the hot whispers about it circulating around town, they told him to scrap Harlem and write the Gate. It was doubtful that Zion had needed much encouragement.

I arrived at Mailer's, paper in hand, around ten. He was lying on the couch in a pair of khaki pants and socks, looking rested. I flipped him the paper, and after reading a few lines he looked up. "That bastard," he shot out. "He told me all day yesterday in the car how much he liked the speech, and now he does something like this. Not a word about Harlem, that bastard." He was looking for sympathy, but I didn't offer any. "I wouldn't have been that easy on you," I said. Mailer was genuinely shocked. He still thought I had liked the speech.

Patiently, I went into a long explanation of how the kids couldn't differentiate between themselves and those whom he'd insulted, and that he had been genuinely scary. He didn't want to talk about it. Instead, he told me how the sights of Harlem had moved him—the incredible squalor of the tenements, the plight of the people. "You have to walk inside one of those tenements to believe it," he continued. Once again, I found myself moved by his awesome compassion, and my mission began to slip from my mind. But like an overdue bill, I presented myself again.

I told him he had done everything those cannibalistic bastards had expected of him. He hadn't insulted them, but gave them the show they came to see. And, I demanded, why hadn't he moved among his workers? He replied that he didn't know that was customary, and it was my fault for not instructing him to do it. He was right. I should have corrected him instead of being angry when I looked at his table. Beverly came into the room, and he reached out for an ally: "This guy is bullying me to death." She flatly replied: "I'm with him."

I served up last what had really upset me. "I agree with you," I said, "when you tell leftists they shouldn't call cops pigs. So where do you get off using that word on your audience?" He looked unbelieving: "Did I say that?" "You called them a bunch of spoiled pigs," I answered. Beverly nodded confirmation. Tears welled up in his eyes, and he turned his head and buried it in the couch. I wished I hadn't pushed that far.

Quickly, I tried to pass over it, assuring him that it had only been one bad night, to forget it, and we would put it all together from here on in. We made plans for him to stop at headquarters later in the day, when he could ease the situation with the kids. At the door, I assured him that my criticism implied nothing personal, but was offered in the tradition of avenging parish priests who threaten to damn sinners' souls to hell. He inquired about the petitions, and I told him we hoped to come in around fifteen thousand. He smiled and said: "Imagine, I thought we could easily get fifty thousand." "That's what I love about you," I countered, "your humility." He offered a thought that had occurred to a lot of people since the night at the Gate: "Imagine if I became mayor." It was an open-ended innuendo that no one at present had the courage to explore.

I made light of the situation at headquarters, explaining that it had been one big put-on among Village friends. This explanation didn't really convince anyone, but it bought some time. Meanwhile, I was hustling Breslin over the phone. He, like Pauline, was facing yet another peril because of the *Times* story. He shouted that Mailer would have been killed in his neighborhood if he ever talked that way there. But Breslin also went out of his way to call various members of the staff and apologize for the evening, especially Krakauer, who was now in full bloom as Deirdre of the Sorrows, since I had banished Alexander from the confines of the royal court. I could be the cause of his death, she cautioned. If so, I humbly hoped my spell would be potent enough to reach her, Mailer, Breslin, and an ever expanding list.

Mailer arrived in the afternoon, his spirits and his hair down from their dizzying heights. He was a portrait of repentance, moving about headquarters shaking hands, thanking everyone for his efforts, avoiding mention of "the night" unless trapped, when he would pass it off as a family skeleton to be heroically closeted by our immediate family. His daylight appearance was just what was needed to expel the midnight fantasy. Later, the kids would make jokes about the evening and, indeed, take some pride that they had been in on it. And at a small fundraising party that evening, Mailer with his great gift for alchemy would use the disaster to his advantage, claiming he had merely taken an innocent breather in his inhumane schedule; and everyone had scored him for it, including his "bullying, ex-longshoreman campaign manager." The breasts of the women present swelled with motherly milk, and they poured out their purses to help the much-abused Norman continue his crusade.

After two days' hibernation, Breslin showed up at headquarters. And when he left, he took a shopping bag full of petitions out to Queens to distribute in saloons. Everybody settled down to the drive for the wire. Dave Block, though he missed Gehrig's record, certainly qualified for the Hall of Fame among petitioners when he delivered more than 1,700 signatures.

That Sunday we cut off petitioning and prepared for the tedious, mind-deadening job of filling out assembly and election district numbers next to each signature. Every address lies within a numbered assembly district and a smaller election district. These addresses must be individually checked on Board of Elections maps to find the corresponding districts. It is a slow, blinding process.

About twenty of us worked into the night. The Weinsteins,

the Tullys, Banning, Stokes, Linzer, Friedman, Cummings, "Barry," and a handful of others who just walked in and stayed on became special to me. The drudgery of the evening's work gave a special cachet to those who would endure it. If the Kennedy loyalty test was "Were you with us in West Virginia?" Mailer's would be "Were you with us on petition eve?"

Tully's sheer strength kept us going through the night. I wanted to quit at 3 A.M., but Paul declared: "If you have them trapped, keep them." The men were stripped to T-shirts and were shoeless, padding about in sweaty socks. All except "Barry," that is, who looked impeccable, like a British colonel in charge of a detail of "beasties." The women looked like what the proverbial cat dragged in. And the borough of Queens with its like-numbered streets, avenues, lanes, and roads became our special nemesis. As Tully squinted at the map, he summed up our feelings: "No wonder Lindsay didn't remove the snow. He couldn't fuckin' find it."

Into the midst of this walked Newfield. He sat alone at a table, leafing through petitions. It was one of his rare appearances, but any extra body was a blessing. After a while he came over and handed me a piece of paper. "I took these names off the petitions," he said. "If we list them as supporters, it would make a great ad for next week's *Voice*." He'd given me the names of celebrities, headed by George Plimpton, who'd signed Mailer's and Breslin's petitions. We who were talking about a coalition of left and right, spade and superpatriot—and he handed me George Plimpton! At this point even his appearance offended me. I understood how Hotspur on his field of battle felt when he looked upon the nobleman: "To see him shine so brisk and smell so sweet"; and I began to think Newfield considered the staff uncouth for bringing our smell "betwixt the wind and his nobility." My face hid nothing, and he quickly left. We wrapped it up at 5 A.M.

The next night Linzer, Stokes, Ferris, and another lawyer, Marty Henderson, and I bound the petitions at Friedman's office. We went to 4 A.M., but at the end we had 14,032 names neatly and legally bound. On the following day Mailer and Breslin cradled them in their arms and carried them to the desk at the Board of Elections. Indeed, they were our labor of love, and the only thing left was to sit back and see how many illegitimate bastards our opponents could discover.

Challenges came from two different sources, Badillo and Scheuer, but they were never to be pursued. The reason for not following through, we learned after talking to aides in both camps, was that though they had had intentions of fighting us all the way, they changed their minds when they saw "that fuckin' screwball perform at the Gate."

So, by an act of midnight madness, we were home free—unchallenged and on the ballot. Hearing the news, we mere mortals were repentant. We had forgotten that the gods work in mysterious ways.

4

The Conversion of the Jews?

THE VILLAGE GATE proved to be an unshakable hangover for Mailer and thus for the campaign. In reality, what was lost that evening was a handful of workers and quite a few potential contributors. Zion's story hurt, but not to the degree Mailer liked to believe. After all, the piece had run two short columns, fewer than 500 words, and was cached midway in the paper where only the most tenacious news ferreters dig. Besides, if our mystical coalition of left and right was as hip as we hoped, anyone in it wouldn't be back wading in that inky sea in the first place; though if they did venture over their heads, the performance as mildly reported shouldn't even have singed their cool.

What was much more damaging and real was a poll that appeared in the New York *Daily News* stating that 60 percent of the voters canvassed *had never heard* of Norman Mailer and Jimmy Breslin. So our problem seemed insurmountable—in a month we had to make the candidates' presence known throughout the boroughs. If we could achieve this, we hoped there would then be some curiosity on the voters' part to know more about them. Of course, the information most easily available would be zany legend, which would again bring us full circle to the one constant in the campaign: "Are they serious?"

So our strategy shifted to one of exposure. Walking tours,

major street rallies, appearances at block festivals and sporting events—wherever crowds gathered in large numbers and were susceptible to the instant baptism of recognition. Of course, our ace in the hole was the media. It was the one game in town where the deck was stacked in our favor. The other candidates had the money to ante up for its use, but the hands they held were dull and predictable. We had the best bluffers at the table, and the play was free—even more so after the Gate. The press was horny with expectation—Jesus, what would *they* do next!

We began utilizing the sixth-hour news by calling formal press conferences to release our position papers. The first of these was on air pollution. Mailer, Manso, and Glenn Paulson of the Scientists Committee for Public Information composed a paper that largely was lacking in depth and distinguished only by two demands: a ban on passenger cars in midtown Manhattan and Mailer's monthly purifier of the air and soul, Sweet Sunday.

But, emotionally, we all were plunging on the television debates. The confrontation between Mailer and the rest. The indistinguishable others who stood pat together. We hoped to dazzle them. After all, didn't we have the ace and the joker rolled into one?

The first debate, sponsored by WPIX, the television station of the *Daily News*, was scheduled for May 15. All the candidates accepted the challenge, including one John Seder from Staten Island, who out of the perennial blue had delivered 7,500 signatures to the Board of Elections on the last filing day. He added an aura of mystery to the confrontation, but we felt little else. Once again, all our vaunted brainpower was dead wrong.

Newfield, Maas, Ferris, Linzer, Dave Garth (Lindsay's television producer), Jeff Greenfield (a former RFK aide now with Lindsay), the candidates, and I met in Mailer's living room to prepare for the debate. Garth and Greenfield were friendly with

Breslin and Newfield, with the common string in the quartet being Robert Kennedy.

The group sat around having drinks and making malicious political small talk while we waited for Adam Walinsky, who had flown up from West Virginia at Breslin's request. Newfield and Maas were upset by the size of the gathering, feeling that Walinsky would be put off by a large congregation; but I wasn't sympathetic to their complaints after Walinsky's dollar delivery at Whyte's restaurant. Anyhow, those who were present had been of constant value to me in the campaign and were not to be banished to give comfort to a flashy import.

Walinsky arrived, and the session began. Garth instructed Mailer in what by now must be television's political canon: "Don't debate your opponent. Look straight at the camera and talk to the people 'out there.'" So much for Richard Nixon's strange legacy to media.

Greenfield suggested Mailer's theme should be his divorcement from the system. It should be our strategy, he plotted, to lay the collective ills of this city on the sagging shoulders of Wagner, Procaccino, *et al.* Mailer should be the average Joe's David against the bureaucratic Goliath. Greenfield delivered an impressive analysis without any frills for his own ego. The situation was presented and a philosophy offered, all in a terse, intelligent style. In its own way it was dazzling, yet short—very American, like the fifty-yard dash. Indeed, Greenfield seems typically American to me—the highly touted rookie who may be called up to bail out the long, sad season of our soul. He is what makes our political life durable, a Whiz Kid in the wings. I asked him to supply me with whatever uncomplimentary facts he had on the Wagner administration, and he said he would. Then, others in the room offered a few suggestions, mostly on issues.

Walinsky had been waiting to strut his moment like an eager

ingenue, but when his time finally came, we got fable instead of fact. He had ridden to Brooklyn Heights in a cab, he related, and as he passed a handsome old house up the street from Mailer's, he commented to the cabdriver on its loveliness. He let his tale hang a moment for dramatic impact. Then he continued with EMPHASIS: "Do you know what that cabdriver said to me? He said, 'It won't be so lovely when the niggers move in!'" Walinsky then leaned forward like a trained seal readying to mount a ball. He was set to pounce upon his point. "And that's where this election is at," he declared. "Black and white!"

Mailer looked at me and mumbled something polite, as to how Walinsky had a point. The rest of the people in the room started to mumble, too, till Breslin played the acolyte and shouted: "Everybody shut up and listen to Adam." Adam then said he saw three major points in the election and began to tick them off. But he didn't get beyond the second, because he had never had three points thought out in his head. Breslin had secured the floor he so coveted, and he was going to do anything, including filibuster, to hold it.

Suddenly, Mailer's politesse, like Walinsky's third point, vanished. He wanted to know whether Walinsky believed in our program: the fifty-first state and the dilution of central power into the neighborhoods. Walinsky hedged, and it was obvious he couldn't care less about our platform. But with Breslin cheerleading his advice, he still was King of the Hill and tried one more gambit. It proved one too many. He told Mailer that his main problem was his image, the doubts about his seriousness as a candidate. It was an old chestnut to the campaign, but at least we all agreed. The remedy he pulled out of the fire was something else. To forever still the idea that Mailer was some kind of oddity, Walinsky insisted that on television Mailer must "look the same as the other guys."

Walinsky made a grave error: Norman Mailer wasn't put on

earth to sing in a chorus. "Kiss a cocksucker," he spat into the stunned silence, "and you'll end up one." The meeting quickly and nervously broke up.

Newfield, Maas, and Walinsky caucused near the kitchen and called Mailer aside. They argued that Walinsky couldn't perform before such a crowd (an odd argument since he had done 80 percent of the talking: perhaps a more honest one would have been that he felt he was slumming with amateurs) and asked Mailer to join them for dinner. He accepted, and I returned to finish up some work at headquarters.

Mailer's driver accompanied them to dinner and later told me of the proceedings. From his account, they were brief. Over drinks Walinsky dramatically told Mailer he would be happy to advise him if he could answer one question: Why did Mailer want to be mayor? Mailer just kept looking down into his drink. The question was repeated two or three times without response. Then Walinsky added an appendage: If Mailer didn't answer the question, he would fly back to West Virginia that evening, not remaining in the city for the debates. By his continued silence, Mailer let it be known they finally had reached a common ground.

Walinsky's appearance was in a strange way illuminating to me, for it made me look at Mailer more closely. The first meeting at Whyte's could be dismissed, since Walinsky knew nothing about the campaign. It also is reasonable to assume he thought Mailer's drive could be highly financed, since he certainly is known in parlors where money congregates. And the expenditure of money in a campaign that has it isn't in itself a guarantee of passage to Hades. What was most disturbing about Walinsky was his disrespect for the electorate. His adman's idea of "the little people," the stogie-chewing cabbie who hates niggers, and his strategy of duping the boobs in television land by looking like the other guy and issues be damned. The disappointment was so acute, because Walinsky's reputation promised a new canvas with bold lines taking uncharted and unexplored directions in our landscape; but when you unwrapped him, he was predictable as a politician's paint-by-the-numbers set.

On the other hand, Mailer had resisted the adopted glamor of Adam's presence, a glamor to which I, as another political novice, also had been vulnerable. Mailer remained his own man and would sing his dark tune no matter how offensive it was to the collective ear. What is generally misunderstood about Mailer is that his many midnight rides against America are taken in the spirit of Paul Revere, a cry, an alarum to his countrymen. Unlikely as it may seem, the man in the saddle is a patriot.

Indeed, Mailer's fault was the opposite of Walinsky's. He had fallen head over heels in love with the voters of New York. The thick ankles, the bad breath, and the acne were nonexistent. Mailer had let down the hair and taken the glasses off the plain Jane and, Shazam! A beautiful broad. It was a sentimentality that at times caused us to waste our energies in areas hostile to us and to map wrongheaded strategy which cost us votes. But isn't an unabashed valentine preferable to a computer-calculated seduction plot? Such philosophical ruminations convinced me that I was managing the right corner.

During these days, Mailer was working harder than ever but enjoying it less. A puritanical, repentant air now hovered over the campaign. It seemed that he was trying to blot the Gate incident from public memory by working harder than any other candidate. But by purging his demons, he also banished his devil-may-care campaign style, a style that many New Yorkers had begun to enjoy. And since the opposition's pieties fell short of godliness, an authentic merry devil was to be cherished.

Mailer was fond of telling audiences that he was running farther to the left and to the right than any man in town. Indeed, at times you felt he would meet himself coming and going. But after the Gate, his angle bent acutely to the right. He began to complain that "too many beards" were accompanying him on his walking tours. Even my beard was one of the "too many." Leftists and their causes became objects of scorn. He wanted to get out and talk to the "real people." All of this seemed an attempt to convince the working class that even though Mailer had played the boy of the Western world at the Gate, deep down old Norm was a regular guy.

He became indifferent to issues that normally would have moved him. It was in this way that Newfield, who was attuned to the causes we should champion, was invaluable. On two occasions, his initial persuasion moved Mailer to take a stand where silence would have been an embarrassment to our effort.

The first was when Brooklyn district attorney Eugene Gold ordered an early morning arrest raid of twenty Black and Puerto Rican students from Brooklyn College. His charge was that the students were plotting to physically destroy the school. The raid clearly constituted breaches of civil liberties: the hour of the arrests, detectives gaining admittance to homes under false pretenses, the leaking of "evidence" to the press (revolutionary writings of Che and Mao were found in some of the students' homes), and finally, an outrageous bond of $15,000 per student. After considerable hassling about taking any stand, Mailer reacted, or overreacted, in his best "further to the left" tradition. Not only did he call for Mayor Lindsay to set up a committee of inquiry to explore the cases and arrests of the students, but he also demanded an investigation into the cases of twenty-one Black Panthers who had been arrested two months earlier in an alleged plot to blow up certain Manhattan department stores. Mailer's issued statement asked: "Why would Black people wish to bomb stores where their own people shop? Why were students arrested in the middle of the night? Who can be certain there are not people working to excite and terrify New

York with the fear of terrorism?" He flatly surmised: "The case smacks of provocateurs!"

The second instance occurred when Black and Puerto Rican parents were conducting a sit-in at Manhattan borough president Percy Sutton's office to protest a school decentralization bill authored by John Marchi, a conservative state senator from Staten Island who was challenging Lindsay for the mayoral nomination in the Republican primary. The Albany legislature had passed the Marchi bill into law, but the parents felt it was a dilution of their demands for community control. Newfield wrote a statement supporting them and tried to induce Mailer to appear at the sit-in. Mailer refused. Newfield then enlisted my support for his request.

I was in sympathy with Newfield, since what had first attracted me to this campaign was the notion of power to the neighborhoods. I told Mailer that we would be no less than liars if we didn't defend the parents' fight. During the drive down to the Civic Center, he raged at Newfield and me about "fuckin' leftist causes" and charged that his campaign was becoming a liberal crusade. Once again, he said he wanted to confront the "real people," whose location, like Mrs. Calibash's, was in some undiscovered domain of the mind—Hello, wherever you are.

We were greeted by a young woman who directed us to Sutton's office and told us what groups were present. One was the Black Panthers. Mailer snarled at me: "You fuckin' asshole." Inside the office, sitting on folding chairs and long tables, were ladies with faces showing enough strength for two revolutions. Mailer obviously liked them on sight. And when the applause rose as he walked to the podium, something like a love affair began. He read his statement into a microphone and was interrupted by frequent handclapping. Near the end of the prepared text, there was a line about how he "*could* appeal to Mayor

Lindsay on this matter." But the passion was bubbling, and cautionary "coulds" were the language of escorts, not lovers, so Mailer shouted: "I not only could, but *will*...." The vaults of heaven cracked.

Back in the car we rode him about his revision in the script. He begrudgingly admitted that Newfield had been right and said he was pleased with the appearance. Then Mailer vehemently stressed that he had learned his greatest political lesson back in 1948, when he saw what the "fuckin' Communists did to Henry Wallace." It was such an incredible pitch no one in the car knew how to handle it.

The next day two Black mothers who had been at the sit-in came to headquarters and volunteered to work. My elation, I must admit, was not dimmed by Norman Mailer's history lesson nor by Henry Wallace's tragedy.

"Life is unfair," said Jack Kennedy. "The gods are also," Norman Mailer might have added.

All of Mailer's newfound sobriety and somberness went unrewarded. In fact, it was scorned. If his campaign was not favored, it at least was bestowed with beguiling flair when he went about his own business. When his "reformation glittered o'er his fault," he went unnoticed. The gods, it seems, withhold grace from counterfeiters.

A telling incident occurred the evening before the debates. Mailer and Breslin had been invited to speak to the Greenwich Village Neighbors for Peace at P.S. 41 on West 11th Street. Mailer felt this would give him an excellent chance to recoup his losses at the Gate. A serious confrontation with Villagers on the issue of the war and how it related to the dread of our city. An impressive performance not only could win back many votes he had alienated at the Gate, but with the press in attendance, he could show that the Village wasn't just a place he came to play. He could do serious work there, too.

He had researched the defense budget and computed what equal spending could produce in the cities in the areas of housing and education, as well as writing a moving text to deliver that night. It began like this: "In the last ten years we have spent 551 billion dollars on defense. The sum is equal to what has been spent in the same number of years on housing and education by federal, state, local, and private sources. Meanwhile, our cities, close to inoperative, heavy, sullen, dangerous as wads of oil-soaked rags, wait for conflagrations and massive applications of law and order to follow, that law and order which will produce sabotage and underground movements in reaction. The specter of a hundred cities as corrupt, as occupied, and as unsettled as Saigan is near to us. Yes, the economic condition of this country is kin to a junkie who depends on the military-industrial complex for a fix. So, just as the children of an addict wither or run wild, so do cities accelerate into their poverty, their rebellions, and their ongoing sense of dread." He was geared for a win. What happened was that he was stopped early on a technical knockout.

Before he arrived, the school auditorium had been seized by a Village organization known as the Crazies. Its members are all young, a collection of sinister children who, under the guise of spreading the pollen of life, offer the midnight mushroom. One cannot conceive who sired them, unless it was the sins of the sixties. The dead, dusty egg of fallout fertilized by the hot sperm of napalm. No matter how they frolic among us, their creative plaything is death.

They mobbed the stage and stood on the seats. Volleyball was played with balloons, the participants standing in different aisles. Games of catch were played across the breadth of the auditorium. Whistles blew, Vietcong flags were unfurled, paper planes flew in formation to airborne shouts of "Kill for Peace," "Bomb the

Pentagon," "Free the Panthers," and "Ho, Ho, Ho Chi Minh, the NLF is gonna win."

Mailer tried to speak, but it was futile. The Crazies sang, shouted, and insulted. "Fuck you, Norman," one yelled. "Liberals like you gave us Nixon." That seems to be the Crazies' canon—liberalism is the enemy. The appearance of change is intended to delay the impending revolution. Their "guerrilla theater" always is reserved for nice, mannerly, liberal audiences. The reason for this, one assumes, is that any group which cherishes free speech so much that they would allow shouts of "fire" in a crowded theater certainly would allow a chorus of "fuck yous" at a political meeting. They know their enemy.

Mailer tried to rouse the others in the audience to throw out the Crazies so he could speak. But such rowdiness was beyond them. When his hecklers brought a V.C. flag on stage, Mailer warned that if it wasn't removed, he would leave. They taunted him about leaving. To compound his bad luck, Mailer mistook the Crazies for their equally deformed twin, a group called the Motherfuckers. He tried once more: "If I can't speak here tonight, I'm prepared to say the CIA has infiltrated the Motherfuckers." Prophetically, he told the audience that though he was only calling the organization by its proper name, the press would accuse him of using obscenities. The next day, the "liberal" New York *Post* had at him once again. A story on the incident ended: "Shouting obscenities at his tormenters, Mailer finally walked out." Such treatment brought one to a philosophical reappraisal: Were the Crazies so crazy?

But the evening wasn't a total loss yet. Mailer was tendered a chance to pull it out. Over 100 people had gathered outside the school to wait for him. They said they still wanted to hear him speak, and someone suggested the park at Union Square and 14th Street. Mailer started to make his move uptown, and the crowd pursued in Pied Piper fashion. It was the kind of incident the press could turn into campaign legend: a beleaguered Mailer, with a lighting assist from the moon, mounting a wooden park bench to purge his tormenters and rally his loyal band. Could Robert Emmett have asked for more?

Mailer walked, secure from the crowd, his flanks protected by Bill Walker (who now and forevermore saw himself in the role of bodyguard) and one of Walker's friends whom I didn't know. This one was fascinating, a beautiful relic. His looks, his clothes, his swagger, his swept-back, lightning-fast hairstyle trapped him in a time machine of the fifties. He was a perfect double for that decade's celluloid Saturday's hero, John Derek. When I tried to reach Mailer's side, he held me a safe knife's length away. It seemed Walker had a costar. And the candidate looked snug as a small afterthought between this burly parenthesis. Spotting my plight, Walker granted me passage with a reassuring nod to his comrade. I introduced myself by name and function and offered my hand. As hep as a snatch of Mickey Spillane dialogue, he shot back: "I'm Johnny Machine."

But when we reached the park, Mailer went right on by. Back on the stage at P.S. 41, a modly dressed Black had passed him a card with an address on it and told him he could hold his "meeting" there. When we arrived at the "meeting hall," it turned out to be a bar, one of those terribly "now" establishments that breathlessly live for the moment. Tarot cards dominated the motif, and the unisex swingers' conversation reduced God's gift to matching pegs and holes. Mailer took a table, not seeming to notice that his followers had been turned back at the door and asked to settle for a nose-to-the-window view of the exalted.

The next day at headquarters, a young lady with aristocratic bearing and a pantry philosophy of politics presented me with a copy of Edwin O'Connor's novel *The Last Hurrah* for Mailer. Inside was a venomous note, stating that she had been among his armies of the night before and suggesting that he might do well to learn something about politics from the mythical Irish mayor of the book. When I presented her gift to Mailer, he promptly shelved it. Any hint that he didn't possess Celtic street grace was a sacrilege of the highest order.

On the evening of the debate Mailer, Banning, and I held a cram session in an office in the Daily News Building on East 42d Street. I had obtained negative information about the opposition from the staff and written it on index cards, and the two of us quizzed Mailer. When he had all the facts down pat, he was made up for the cameras and led to a glass-enclosed foyer to pose with the other candidates for news photographers.

For garrulous public men, they had little to say to each other. They exchanged curt handshakes and smiles so forced it seemed as if it had taken a tug-of-war of the cheeks to produce them. Similar to pro football players, they were psyching themselves rather than their opponents.

Badillo was no surprise; his appearance remained a crisp constant. Mario was his opposite, small and round with a manicured anchovy of a mustache on his upper lip; not one whose voice would reach the penthouses of Manhattan, but a street singer to be reckoned with.

Scheuer could be one of Philip Roth's Short Hills, New Jersey, Jews—muscular and pampered at the same time. He moves with a limp, a leftover from a childhood illness, and has a big, boyish face with heavy eyebrows. When angered during the debate, his eyebrows became storm clouds, and the face shifted darkly as if shot through a Wellesian lens, rendering a portrait of a man capable of raising Kane.

And the touted heavyweight, Wagner. His face and quivering hands were mottled with liver spots, the washy blue eyes irretrievably at sea. The smallness of the man, the valiant attempt of his hair to cover his skull, and his little boy feet neatly tucked into a highly polished pair of back-to-school black shoes. For truth-in-packaging he should have been labeled FRAGILE. But the crowd in the room focused on him. He had perishable star quality, and like Garland, his drama was his impending disintegration.

On Seder, the light horse, judgment would tarry till he took the track.

Nobody except the candidates was allowed in the studio. Each candidate was to be allotted two minutes for an opening statement, and they drew lots to determine the speaking order: Scheuer, Seder, Mailer, Procaccino, Wagner, and Badillo. Good for Scheuer and Badillo; everyone else was lumped into the indistinguishable middle.

Scheuer set the tone for the debate by immediately addressing himself to the problem of crime. Law and order would be the umbilical cord that held all the debates together and often made them sound like a sheriffs' convention. Scheuer also tried to pass that valuable coin of the political realm, the Kennedy name. He said that he and Ted had sponsored a bill to recruit the federal government's aid in fighting crime in the cities. He concluded that he would bring "effective, shirtsleeves, working leadership to the city." It was a deft toss, producing two heads—Teddy's and Bobby's.

The camera panned in on Seder, and the media found a new messenger. One could sense that lethargic spines were being straightened in the chairs in television land. Tall, lean, good-looking, wearing a no-nonsense business suit that was respectably dated, Seder sported a blond crew cut. The crew cut was the touch: a man without frills. A team man. One who could quarterback for NASA or the Baltimore Colts, a lanky Johnny U. And when Lee Nelson, the moderator, called "time in," Seder marched the length of the field: "Some weeks ago we saw pictures in the papers of families dressed in rags living in miserable shacks, children with distended bellies. Some of these pictures were from Biafra, some of these pictures were from South Carolina. And we New Yorkers thought, 'Well, South Carolina, what can you expect from a backward place like that?'

"I suggest that hunger is closer to home than you may realize. This summer, in New York City, there will be hunger and malnutrition as a result of the welfare cuts enacted in Albany last month. Think about what that means. Think about a mother trying to explain to a crying two-year-old that there is no milk, no food, and the next check is three days away. Think about that most magnificent of all the works of almighty God, the human brain, stunted and dwarfed, its full growth stopped by protein insufficiency in the early years of life. This brain damage is permanent. It can never be corrected. And this will happen this summer in this greatest city of this wealthiest and most powerful nation in the world, a nation that calls itself civilized.

"I entered this campaign with these five good men, each with his own special talents and abilities and experience, because I didn't feel that I heard from them the sense of urgency about the enormous crisis that faces this city."

When he had finished, the opposition was a shambles. By some manner of clandestine consent, the others had come to brawl in the gutter, only to have their rumble turned into a clean fight by this political Jack Armstrong. Their forays against one another now would seem niggling and petty. By comparison with Seder, all became suspect, four by their profession and Mailer by his mere presence. They were indicted without a hearing, like the man who was asked, "How *do* you beat your wife?"

Mailer hadn't missed the implication. He graciously tossed a bouquet to Seder, and then he spoke of the malnutrition that concerned him: "Mr. Seder's words were quite moving, and I agree with him that there's going to be enormous hunger in this city this summer. There's also going to be a continuing sense of another kind of hunger, which is a spiritual hunger." He expanded his theme by saying that besides the problems of law and order and welfare, there were problems "the experts sometimes call alienation and anomie."

Whatever it was called, alienation or plain unhappiness, it was the rock on which Mailer built his church. Even as he articulated more issues throughout the campaign than any other candidate (he issued more than 18,000 words in position papers on major urban problems), his campaign grew inward, past where the body could legislate. A Badillo aide would angrily say to me later: "Why doesn't your man talk issues and cut out all that Elmer Gantry bullshit?"

Mailer concluded his two minutes with a plea for the fifty-first state and declared he was the only one who could bring it about (an exception was made for Seder), because he was "an amateur," and "a promise from any of the others would take twenty-two years to fulfill." The statehood portion of his remarks was delivered in a stuffy, purse-lipped style with an accent an ocean removed from his native Brooklyn. This British accent, added to his navy pinstripe suit and vest, would forever mute thoughts of his frivolity. Mailer was a homebred Harold Macmillan.

Murray Kempton saw it differently in his New York *Post* column the following day: "... from the fear of not being thought serious, [Mailer] is lugubrious; he looks indeed like Lady Chatterley's father without the sense of humor."

One expected a humble entrance from Procaccino, a professed man of the people; but instead he proudly popped up like a buxom broad out of a birthday cake. "There's no question in my mind," he said, "who is the best qualified to save the city of New York. I will serve with courage, energy, dedication, and tremendous experience." He posed for the cameras: "Look me over. You're looking at a man who has been.............." (He listed an endless tapeworm of his jobs and accomplishments, only excluding what must have been miraculous valor when he faced vaccination.) It was a ludicrous performance.

Wagner's antiquity was priceless. He sauntered into this room of brash alarmists who spoke of starving children, strange-sounding afflictions beginning with *a*'s, and crisis, and he quizzically looked around him as if to say, "What the hell is all this about?" Wasn't his presence enough? Wasn't the Old Champ (as the press was fond of calling him) back in the ring? He talked of how people had come up to him in the streets—the housewives, the hackies—and asked him "to come back, please." Sure, he had had a vacation, he went on, every mayor should have one, and now he intended to give John Lindsay his. He recalled how smoothly things had gone when he was in City Hall: garbage collected, subways running, and races united. He cast a cold eye on Lindsay and the zealots who flanked him tonight, these Democratic defilers of antiques. "But things haven't changed that much," he assured, "that you have to discard everything for the sake of change."

It was a remarkable performance. He had managed to transform his opponents into ranting Cassandras. Only he could lull the city. He would return everybody to a peaceful trance, because only he knew the beat of the important pulses in town. He would conduct a municipal seance, with the hands of everybody who mattered under the table.

Badillo also began by laying out his credentials, but unlike Procaccino, he did it in a matter-of-fact, understated fashion. Born in Puerto Rico, a graduate of CCNY and Brooklyn Law School, a lawyer, a CPA, and currently borough president of the Bronx. It was a modest beginning for a man who would not promise to make New York a great city, only a livable city. Mailer felt it betrayed the breadth of Badillo's soul.

Badillo was easily the best of the borough presidents, and he capitalized on this by next itemizing his accomplishments in the Bronx, which was a lead into his campaign philosophy, that he was fit to govern because "the Bronx is a microcosm of the city of New York." It was an innocuous strategy, yet dangerous, since it presupposed the militant identity of the other boroughs. Did the cliff dwellers of Manhattan, those big-town sharps high on the scale of the "Symphony of the City," want to be toned down to a Bronxite flat? Did those legends of elocution in Brooklyn, who made the corner of "Thoity-Thoid Street and Thoid Avenue" famous throughout the world, want the Grand Concourse to become their Pygmalion? Surely, Badillo was a square Puerto Rican—he had violated the city's cherished concept of "turf."

But his statement was neat and precise, and perhaps such an unadorned man was exactly what the city was looking for. I found it difficult to judge Badillo's performance, since I was not without preconceptions of the man. I respected him for his decency, efficiency, and appetite for hard work. But to me, he was not a man to lead New York. His weaknesses were Lindsay's weaknesses, based on a philosophy nurtured in bureaucratic liberalism. His edge over Lindsay would be in administration and efficiency, but he seemed to lack the mayor's major strength, the embodiment of urban America.

What is overlooked in Lindsay, a man known primarily for his street presence in the ghetto, is that he also is a symbol to the new breed of young, middle-class, familied whites, a symbol who scorns the Babylons and the Levittowns and seductively creates a yen for the subway. And without these families, the city is lost, left to those in the inner circle who come to play and to those in the widening ripples who are doomed by their conditions to stay. To me, Badillo was not enough. If decency is the only prerequisite for leadership, why then weren't all the saints Michael?

The very format of the first debate and the ones that followed was so truncated that a meaningful exposure of ideas would never occur. The minimal allotment of time to each candidate (Do two-minute wind sprints afford adequate insights into the man who the experts claim must fill "the second toughest job in America"?) allowed for only skeleton platforms, shadowy accusations, flimsy rebuttals, and creaky humor.

The distinguishing aspect of this first meeting was that Procaccino responded emotionally and shouted at Scheuer when the congressman questioned the integrity of one of the controller's aides. But, the viewer might ask, wasn't this the same emotionalism that had moved the man to obtain a court order to open City College a month earlier, when the campus was seized by Black and white radicals demanding an open admissions policy? To many, including the large Jewish community whose sons and daughters dominate the student body, wasn't his "emotionalism" really courage when it was pitted against the permissive "coolness" of the others who allow *them* to have their own way?

The second highlight was Mailer's attempt at a quick kayo of the Old Champ. Using the factual ammunition we had supplied him, he attacked Wagner for having left the city one-quarter billion dollars in debt on his departure and called the Wagner administration "limp and complacent." But the most damaging blow came when Mailer pointed out that Wagner had failed to return from a vacation in Spain when the Harlem riots broke out in 1964, even though there was loss of life and property. The charge riddled Wagner's image as the Manager, the man who could cool a crisis with a phone call. And in a city accustomed to John Lindsay walking angry streets, it said little for Wagner's courage.

With a facial expression as bland as oatmeal, Wagner rebutted him. He said he didn't know if Mailer was "really serious" about running for mayor or not: "He's getting a good deal of publicity on it, but I would just like to straighten out a few facts." He noted that the riot had been in 1965, not 1964, that he had flown back immediately, and that there had been no loss of life.

Mailer, who liked to bandy about his own amateurism, didn't

trust that status in his researchers and meekly kept silent. Perhaps it was just another facet of his Americanism: when in doubt, buy the proven product.

Immediately, a phone call from Breslin was put through to me. Not only had the riots occurred in 1964, he said, they were sparked when a Black teen-ager was shot to death by a patrolman outside Robert F. Wagner High School on the upper East Side of Manhattan! "Get in that studio and tell that son of a bitch," Breslin roared. But the studio was locked to outsiders, and Mailer, now shaken, admitted Wagner was right about the date of the riot.

It was an incredible move. If he was unsure of the facts we had given him, he should have remained silent and let the incident pass. But to grant Wagner the benefit of the doubt, openly and publicly when it wasn't demanded, was ludicrous. The spiritual message Mailer finally managed to convey in this first encounter was that the bout between David and Goliath must have been fixed.

With primary day roughly a month away, money still was a major problem. Mailer continued to write his own checks, and on many days the operation, like a poor parish church, relied strictly on the contents of the (button) basket. Of course, there were the small fund-raising parties, affairs usually hosted by the barnacles of the Beautiful People.

Most often, they were held in cramped (or perhaps we should say intimate) apartments on the east side of Central Park. The setting and the troop always were the same, a losers' repertory. The hostess invariably was clad in lounging pajamas with bare feet and was as emotionally sticky and all-encompassing as a melted marshmallow. The furniture was the same variety they had mocked in their mothers' houses, but now the rebellious daughters adorned it with bright, casual throws and pillows. By their manner, these ladies obviously thought their sleight of hand was a success, but it would have taken a Houdini to disguise these overstuffed elephants. The kitchen housed the liquor, which usually looked like the remnants of a party instead of the beginning—always vodka and scotch with names so obscure you didn't remember if the vodka was named after a clan and the scotch after a count or vice versa. For the robust of appetite, there were the standard four bowls, two of potato chips, two of pretzels.

The candidate would be dragged out into the middle of the living room to make his speech and his spiel. At this precise moment, the young reformers present would adjust their glasses with elaborate seriousness, straighten their jackets, tighten their mod ties, and heft the checkbooks in their breast pockets for presence, as one checks all airy objects. The hostess would take her honored place, sitting cross-legged on the floor at the candidate's feet, gazing upward with a look that only stalks the back streets of Fanny Hurst novels.

Mailer would delve into philosophy and platform, the young men would nod, and the ladies would be bursting with attention. At the end, there was nervous coughing, much maneuvering for the bedroom where the coats were, and swift exits preceded by such remarks as "He's charming, but not as mayor," or "I'm sorry, darling, but I can't take your man seriously." Those who did contribute almost always went for five dollars, not much of a tariff considering they had met a Pulitzer Prize winner, drunk four scotches, had some sustenance (no matter how meager or how greasy), and had a chance to meet the opposite sex to create what is known in these circles as "a very meaningful relationship." Our sheer presence in such rooms darkly convinced me that even in the fifty-first state, God was losing.

But if money was a problem, personnel luckily was not. For salaries that would just about cover ordinary living expenses, I was able to add three more members to the staff. Tully recommended the first, Whit Smith, one of his Yale classmates and a co-worker in the Lowenstein campaign. Smith's strength was supposed to lie in research and the formulation of difficult detailed position papers. We needed such a strength. The biggest gap in our fifty-first-state proposal was precise proof that it would be financially beneficial to be free from Albany; and if it would, how much the new state would gain and from what sources. We also wanted to know what we could do with the additional revenue in terms of services, complementary equipment, housing, etc. When this particular document finally was drafted, it became known throughout headquarters as Smith's Shopping List because of the assorted goodies it offered.

Alcott Whitman Smith. The very name gave a hint of the WASPish wealth of his New England family; his appearance did not. Whit's costume was not beat, hippie, or Yippie, since it didn't posture in its poverty or nonconformity. It was an ensemble without ego. Like the rest of his clothes, his dungarees were freshly laundered, but they also were shot through with holes. The shoes, constantly gregarious with their bottoms loosely flapping up and down. A faded blue work shirt was stuffed down into the dungarees, at the waist of which a piece of rope of the most common variety held the whole ensemble together like a hobo's pack. Indeed, only the bygone word "hobo" suited him, for at twenty-three years of age, his clothes offered nothing contemporary but evoked the unpretentious squareness of the boxcar.

Like many on the staff, Smith offered the bonus of his wife's services. Gilvy Smith, like her husband, was gentle in face and temperament, part of that national treasure we as a country discovered on campus during the late winter and early spring of 1968. And for decorative innocence at headquarters, they brought their baby son, who was menacingly nicknamed "Bubba" after the Baltimore Colts' huge defensive end "Kill, Bubba, Kill" Smith.

With them came another Smith, but no relation. Because we needed someone with experience to set up the planned street rallies (a job now handled by a young volunteer named Paul Schwartzman), I hired Dustin Smith, a man in his late twenties with a head chockful of strawberry blond curls, who had worked as an advance man for Robert Kennedy in his 1964 Senate race.

Through Tully and Whit Smith's recommendations came yet another Lowenstein alumnus, Joel Peister, who had degrees from the University of Pennsylvania and CCNY. Peister has an ebullient personality and bottomless energy that made him the perfect man to coordinate philosophy and supplies between the main headquarters and those in the boroughs. A perfect emissary, with a hairstyle as buoyant as his nature, to spread happiness in the hinterlands.

Some good cheer was needed out in the boroughs, too. Our movement was unlike any previous left campaigns in the sense that we had the young volunteers but no seasoned reformers to guide them. The reform clubs were mostly Badillo's, with a small segment for Scheuer, and a scattering of black humorists for Wagner. Our dilemma was that babes were leading babes.

Gary Pogrow and Allen Stern, two young teachers, were our Bronx coordinators. Their dedication and energy were beyond question, but they were not tied in with any political movement in their borough.

Nobody wanted hostile Queens until a young Californian named Ken Lieberman wandered into headquarters and volunteered on a permanent basis. He had had experience in RFK's final campaign in California. Willing, blond, good-looking in that clean-cut surfer's way, he was ideal for Queens. But besides his appearance, he was optimistic about the borough and didn't realize what hostility awaited him. Such, I suppose, is the mentality of those who ride waves.

Ferris still had Brooklyn, but his strength was in ideas, not command. From time to time, his roving assistant was a dapperish young lawyer, Hilly Gross. Gross is a delight: dry, understated, urbane, and solidly skeptical—a Jewish William Powell.

And, of course, this entire sprawl was to be held together by a campaign manager who would be lost in three of the five boroughs. The thin line between our amateurism and our ignorance quickly was becoming indistinguishable.

With our time getting shorter and no indication that the right wing in the city was responding to our platform of local control in all neighborhoods, we shifted to a traditional strategy, wooing the huge Jewish vote.

Tully began to call synagogues to arrange speaking engagements for Mailer. The response was disheartening and surprising, since we were offering a prized and honored son. Over the last year, the Jews (mainly the teachers) had seen their once cherished relationship with the Blacks split asunder in the New York City schoolteachers' strike over decentralization. Anti-Semitic slurs uttered by Blacks cropped up daily in the papers, and the papers and Albert Shanker, president of the United Federation of Teachers, played it to the hilt.

They had a marvelous tool in Leslie Campbell, a teacher in the Ocean Hill-Brownsville area in Brooklyn, where the decentralization issue was born. Out of thirty-seven articles about Black anti-Semitism that appeared in the newspapers over a period of weeks, a check showed that thirty were attributable to one man—Leslie Campbell.

So, such distortions in the press and by the teachers' union created a paranoia in the Jewish community—the Negroes became ebony reminders that it can happen here.

Mailer's plan for complete community control was not being met with enthusiasm by the Jews either. Control of one's schools meant the choice of one's teachers, which in logical progression meant the demise of the UFT and, in the minds of its predominantly Jewish membership, the resultant decline of "professionalism." Their second argument with Mailer was over his position on letting a ghetto police itself. The same ghettos that fringe so many Jewish neighborhoods. The blackness of his suggestion was as sinister as a squid's ink. Next, of course, was the question of Mailer's Jewishness. He was a Jew who was known to move through a *goyim*'s world of saloons and prizefighters. A man of many wives. A comrade-in-arms to violence. And most deadly, as the Jewish Defense League pointed out, a cash contributor to the enemy—in fact, the apex of the enemy, the Black Panthers.

After Tully's chilly reception, I tried, figuring that perhaps a personal call from "the campaign manager" would carry more clout. I figured wrong. Then, I reasoned, Tully and I were Irishers. By the simple ground rules of city politics, we should have been handling the Hibernian clubs. We started to look for a Jewish emissary. Not any Jew, for we had many with distinguishing characteristics, but a Jew who would be acceptable, one who could visit synagogues to set up speaking engagements and not be remembered specifically for his shaggy hair or his beard but in totality as "a nice Jewish boy." We had only one candidate for the job, Paul Schwartzman. A young man with impeccable manners and grooming, bright but not dazzling, idealistic but not abrasive, who was near the principals and the drama yet removed and unaware. Enter our Rosencrantz and Guildenstern— or was it—

Sad to say, the best all this maneuvering produced was a handful of Jewish groups for speaking engagements and a blatant rejection to tour the hotels in the borscht belt of the upstate Catskill Mountains where many of the Jews spend their summer vacations. It also forbode tidings to come, when the first group to invite us was an isolated community on the fringe of Jamaica Bay in Queens.

Sunday morning, Mailer, Banning, Lee Cook, and I drove to

the Howard Beach Jewish Center. During the drive we talked of the preceding day. Mailer had attended a block party on Berkeley Place in the Park Slope section of Brooklyn. John Scanlon, a resident of the block and one of the party's organizers, had issued the invitation. Mailer had arrived in casual clothes with his mother, two of his daughters, and his and Beverly's two blond sons, Michael and Stephen. Michael, age five, has delicate, aristocratic looks that on one occasion moved Mailer to remark "he could be a sheer beauty." Stephen, age three and less delicate-looking, is his father's companion for roughhouse, equally appreciated for his different gifts.

The scene on the block had moved Mailer: brownstones set on tree-lined streets gently sloping down from Prospect Park; not a sign of a high-rise project; and whites, Blacks, and Puerto Ricans mingling freely on the cordoned-off street, all enjoying franks and beers while their children played a variety of games or raptly watched a pageant being presented on the street. Neighbors of various ethnic persuasions had cooked their own specialties and were selling them from the stoops and front yards. Colorful homemade banners were stretched across the street, attached to houses on opposite sides. Raffles and wheels of chance were in high gear with all the proceeds, as well as the sales of food and drinks, marked for the block association program to plant trees and make general improvements.

To Mailer it was a glance into the Promised Land—his vision of the city in microcosm. Conservative Irish and Italians, young liberals of all stripes, monied WASP's enjoying work and play with aspiring Blacks and Puerto Ricans in a landscape that successfully had resisted the bulldozer. His diminutive mother, a little taken back by the raucousness of it all, cautiously asked, "Do you like it?" With a loving look at the colorful hodgepodge, he buoyantly answered, "It's exactly when I have been talking about. I'm running against urban renewal!"

After the Brooklyn appearance, Mailer had driven his family out to Queens in his Peugeot. His trip, he told us, had taken the edge off his pleasant morning. Recounting the journey, he turned in the front seat and said to a reporter from *Life* magazine who was traveling with us: "When I saw the poverty in Brownsville, I felt like crying, and I said, 'I don't want to be mayor of this evil, evil city.'" Later, when he had got to Queens, he told us he'd experienced a different kind of revulsion, seeing Queens Boulevard with its endless fortresses of garish apartment houses. "I frightened my mother," he said. "When I looked at Queens Boulevard, I said, 'So this is what money has done. Any species that created Queens Boulevard doesn't deserve to exist.'"

By the time we arrived at the temple, Mailer was over his "spiritual miasma" (as he called it) and was anxious to speak to his people. Breslin was waiting, obviously not recovered from the affliction that befell him the night before. His eyes looked as if they were on a weekend pass from an asylum, and his voice was a croak. The temple, like the community, was flat and uninspired. Its architecture was a larger and slightly more elaborate variation on the surrounding ranch houses. It was a community without geography—impermanent, a bivouac set in a desert. And the Jews inside the temple were nomads, a group who seemed to have conditioned themselves to the proposition that their legacy was to flee. For a people steeped in history, they had chosen a resting place that could be removed without trace by an angry wind.

They sat inside at tables. There was a smattering of old men, but no ancients. The younger men were heavy and muscular—handball players perhaps. You wondered how they made their money. Certainly not in swank law offices or glamorous showrooms, by the cut of their clothes. But not on the lower East Side as merchants either. There was no smell here. Anywhere. The cream cheese on the table was a commercial brand; the lox was prepackaged and arranged on paper plates; the coffee cups were styrofoam; and the sacred Jewish plate from which one eats was paper with a serrated edge.

It was Sunday, but the women were not. Monday, maybe Thursday, but not Sunday. They were playing suburban wives, Protestant plain Janes to their husbands' dark-blue-slacked and Banlon-shirted regular Joes. Jews looking for anonymity, a place to rest. Fellow workers and socializers only with other nomads. The nuclei for another Los Angeles. What makes them run?

Breslin was no help. The rabbi took one look at him and announced that "Breslin doesn't reflect the views of this temple." The outsider began by saying he was sorry to break in on them with such harsh words so early in the morning, but the biggest problem in the city was between Black and white. He talked of how angry Blacks in Far Rockaway on the fringe of their community were. Nobody had yet had coffee, and it was ten in the morning, and this wild-eyed Irisher was rasping about race riots. Mailer glared at him; he was having unholy thoughts in a holy house. Obviously, Breslin misunderstood the audience's glacial silence for rapt attention. He continued with how things had so deteriorated that the Blacks were calling the Jews kikes and other despicable names. For the first time he got a reaction, showing nondiscovery—"So, what's new?" He then bellowed that the answer is not "Beat up the *schwartzes*." If paper could rattle, the plates would have.

The rabbi introduced Mailer and with added emphasis said that the guests did not reflect the view of the temple. If Mailer had come alone, it would have been fine. He began talking of his respect for his people and how he had been guilty of ill-spending some time. That was the time that had made the bad gossip. Many were moved, but it was too little too late. Breslin had blitzed them. In effect, he had told them their pilgrimage was in vain; once again the tiger (or was it now the Panther) was at their gates.

Mailer tried everything from confession to discussion of high finance in the fifty-first state, but the questions always came back to local control. Did that mean schools and police, too? Each time, a frightening yes. When he left the podium, one elderly man turned to a younger table mate and said: "If *their* police have guns, what would stop them from coming in and killing *our* police?" No humor should be that black.

As we were leaving, Mailer's natural allies, the ladies, tried to make him feel their meeting had been pleasant. They asked for autographs, flirted ever so slightly, and in a moment of high feeling some took the address of our headquarters, so that they could send an invitation for Mailer to reappear at another gathering two weeks hence. The invitation never came. But, one sadly reflected, they may have been too busy packing.

The second stop of the morning at the Avenue Z Jewish Center in Brooklyn was better. Its location in Brooklyn made it better. No split-levels here. Apartment houses with Flatbush Florentine fountains dominated the terrain. The women, unlike their nomadic sisters, were dressed for a loving kill, and the men's disagreement with the candidates didn't take the form of whispering paranoia, but a healthy ball-park raspberry. The center itself was lush: chandeliers, stained glass windows, solid pews—all donated by members present or departed, their names memorialized on gold plates. Breslin received a good-natured hooting for having insulted Albert Shanker, whose interests, he said, lay elsewhere, since Shanker lived outside the city proper. But it was a mutual perversion. Both sides enjoyed the hell out of it.

Mailer seemed to sense the shift in turf and realized he was home again. In a Moses voice he chided them for berating "a dark-haired, good-looking Irishman with a hangover." Then in a humble switch, he told them he was the embodiment of on-the-job training. As he talked, the yarmulke fell to the floor from Mailer's curly head. An embarrassed silence filled the center; but as Smith used Dale, and Abbott used Costello, Mailer used the deity as second banana. Looking heavenward, he solemnly intoned: "I hope the Lord has not spoken."

Mailer made three more stops that day: two clubs and an address to a group of senior citizens in a high school. He was impressive at all three, and the candidate and his staff ended the day on a high note. Then came Blue Monday.

I arrived at Mailer's house in the late afternoon with spirits flying. It had nothing to do with politics. My wife had just given birth to our second child, Siobhan Maggie, whom Mailer was to christen "the First Lady Baby of the campaign."

Ferris, Manso, and some others were there, working on an upcoming position paper. Mailer broke out a jug, and we hoisted the traditional drink to new life. But I sensed some cutting edge in the room. Mailer seemed to be restraining himself against an outburst of temper.

After a few minutes, he asked if I had seen that afternoon's New York *Post*. I answered that I hadn't, and with a gesture of elaborate disgust he tossed me the paper, which was open to the editorial page column of Washington-based Mary McGrory.

The Friday before, Mailer, Breslin, and Newfield had met with McGrory in the Russian Tea Room on West 57th Street. From a previous McGrory column, it was obvious she was a Scheuer booster, since he had been one of New York City's earliest supporters of Eugene McCarthy. And in the McGrory canon, that constituted divinity by osmosis. It was a meeting that demanded keeping one's guard up. Mailer was obviously aware of this and conducted himself cautiously. But he had to leave early to cover a stop in Brooklyn, and McGrory was left with Breslin and Newfield. And when it came to media, those two left themselves wide open, but not naïvely. Joyously, with their legs straight up in the air.

Breslin ridiculed Mailer's performance in the debates, and

Newfield spoon-fed her quotes. He said Mailer was an uneven campaigner, and "he'd like to be Brendan Behan," referring to Mailer's performance at the Gate; then he rounded out the Gate evening for her by supplying Breslin's quote about "running with Ezra Pound." Breslin, for his part, distorted what Mailer had said about the Jews, that "for twenty years, the politics of the Jews has been dictated from the grave of Adolf Hitler," into a statement that Mailer was going to make a screaming attack on his people. Newfield, I learned, had added at this point that we were going to tell the Jews "Up Against the Torah," a bit of purple overindulgence McGrory didn't use. But all the rest was there in glorious black and white in the city's most influential Jewish newspaper, the daily testament of the people we were trying to convert.

It was now Mailer's chance to do the talking. He and Breslin had gone at it already over the telephone before I arrived. Now Mailer dialed Newfield and asked: "Who the fuck do you think you are, analyzing me in print with that Behan quote?" He told Newfield he had enough enemies and didn't need them on his staff as well. Then he passed the phone to me, saying, "Here's Flaherty."

Newfield and I let go at a civilized roar. I told him he had taken one ego trip too many during the campaign, that he wouldn't have dared to pull this kind of shit on any other candidate with whom he'd been associated. He shouted back that he had only been kidding: Wasn't this campaign supposed to be looser than others? But I wouldn't buy it. The sheer quotability of what he'd said got me. When he delivered those quotes, he had known they would see light.

But I was also being unfair. Newfield singly had begun to represent to me all those who in the beginning had the bad grace to convince Mailer to begin a serious enterprise, one that would expose a valuable man and make him a target for mockery. An enterprise they would instantly abandon or on occasion visit, as one visits a child from a broken marriage, particularly on Sunday when the day-to-day drudgery has disappeared and the object of affection is ready to pose for photographs.

But making Newfield a symbol of all this was not wholly valid. Though he seldom showed, often when he did he brought a cause to champion with him, unlike the others. Too, there had been a grating edge to our relationship ever since the McCarthy-Kennedy holy wars, during which I had hit his politics in print and he had rebutted.

So our phone conversation ended with his slamming down the receiver, a mutual desire on both sides to part company. Thereafter, he restricted himself to advising and traveling occasionally with Breslin, who became, in his eyes, the real class of the ticket. One never knew if this was a paean to Jimmy's street genius or the gutter loyalty one pays an accomplice.

Luckily for the mood of the candidate, his schedule was so heavy he didn't have time to dwell on disasters. During this week, he performed some of the city's political rituals: lunch with the New York *Post* editorial board, a presentation of his platform before the Citizens' Union, a press conference to release a position paper on transportation, an appearance before the Board of Estimate at City Hall to denounce the construction of the Lower Manhattan Expressway, speaking to Women Strike for Peace and the League of Women Voters.

He also appeared in a debate on Channel 13, the city's educational television station, with Badillo, Seder, and Scheuer. Both Wagner and Procaccino had refused to appear before the limited audience, probably thinking correctly that the vote of the station's egghead audience was scrambled among the four gentlemen who accepted. Also, Mario's "little people" might have been offended to find their "regular guy" on such a perverse airway.

For Wagner it was a matter of class—Heifetz doesn't fiddle in parlors.

It also was a week in which Mailer played the political clubs in the distant boroughs until late in the night. And if the day came up sunny, he walked the streets and was not only recognized but quizzed in earnest about the fifty-first state, an idea maverick enough to have some appeal to New Yorkers. His energy was boundless under the worst of conditions. The humidity sapped vitality, and the air pollution was gagging. The sky was a sleazy gray, a tint that fell somewhere between that of a flophouse sheet and the imagined hue of bad breath.

Oddly, the adverse conditions seemed to please Mailer—they were a test of his stamina and a reassurance of his sincerity. At times, he would talk about the toughness of his days, the heat, the brain-deadening repetitive speeches, the fourteen-hour schedule, his voice seemingly a reminder to the Lord to log these days as payment for more frolicking ones.

And like the girl with the curl, when he was good he was very, very good. Boozing was a reward he held off until the end of the night, either when work was done or when he was at a congenial evening fund raiser where an occasional outrageous remark was an asset. And as a campaigner, he was never better. Whether he was telling a young audience about our diminishing national soul or nostalgically recounting to a Puerto Rican club on the lower East Side how he had once lived there and spent a summer rebuilding his own apartment and how he loved it when it was done. And if he was mayor, these people would have the same chance. Indeed, they could under neighborhood sovereignty form co-ops and own their own apartments. Then he puckishly added that the community hippies would have a right to their neighborhood also, and that the others must respect that right, even if "the hippies chose to make love on top of cars." And instead of being outraged, the old Puerto Rican couples howled and raucously poked each other with their elbows, so that no one in the hall would miss what he had said. It was classic Mailer. A potpourri of his conservative "a man and his castle" view, spiced with his outrageous extension of civil and spiritual liberty. But mostly, they responded not to the content of his message but to the honesty of the man. His ideas perhaps were not what they could relate to their own experience, or then again maybe they could. What was more important was that he didn't pander to them or ethnically try to shill them. He honestly liked them, and they him, and he had the bald-faced audacity to tell them what he *really* thought about the city. And among the poor, who have been showered with it, the promised drought of bullshit was most appealing.

It was that Friday that we were crucified once and for all. After a month of turmoil on campus, a team of faculty members and representatives of the Black and Puerto Rican students came up with a dual admissions program for CCNY. In 1970 half of the freshman class would be admitted exclusively from eleven high schools in the depressed and segregated areas of Harlem and the Bronx, while the other half would be chosen according to the traditional academic criteria. Since it meant the refusal of admittance to a number of qualified white students, moreover white Jewish students, the other candidates denounced it as a "quota" system, a word with dark roots in Jewish history.

On the advice of Cliff Adelman, a teacher at the college and the author of our education paper, we endorsed the plan. But even without Adelman's insistence, we would have backed it. A copy of the proposal was delivered to me at headquarters. All our key aides read it, and to a man we voiced our support.

But Mailer didn't wait on our collective advice. To him, it was a matter of instinct: "The moment white boys can't get a free education in this city is the moment we are going to get open admissions for all and community colleges. Not before. So long as Black boys are denied, you're going to have the same buckpassing and complaints about expenses. So that's why I support the dual admissions system." His instinct was to prove prophetic. After the primary, the city instituted an open admissions policy.

But when the heat was on, one and all got out of the kitchen. Except Mailer and Breslin, who reentered the campaign with new vigor. "The kids make this whole thing worthwhile," Breslin said. "Now I am happy I did it."

Mailer scored his opponents for "bleating about law and order" and then exiling the kids to the street. When Lindsay bowed to the pressure, Mailer said it was the first time he had seen the mayor show lack of courage. Badillo, the liberal light, denounced the "quota" system without ever reading the proposal. Murray Kempton told me that Badillo had called him, after Murray had written two columns analyzing the proposal of which he was in favor, to tell him that he had just read it and it wasn't nearly as bad as he had imagined. This was three days after Badillo had issued his denunciation, an action that moved Doug Ireland, one of his young aides, to remark: "I wrote Herman's bilingual literature, English and Yiddish."

But we were to pay dearly for our stand. That Sunday morning at the Briarwood Jewish Center in Jamaica, Mailer was set upon by members of the Jewish Defense League who attacked him for defending the Blacks, who, according to the angry spokesman, "are shitting all over the Jews." Another asked if Mailer, a man who had stabbed his wife, was "stable" enough to be mayor, and summed it up as an obscenity to have such a man as a guest in the synagogue.

Instead of cringing, Mailer ran right into their teeth. He not only defended his educational stand but attacked any Jew who rented a slum or operated a "schlock shop" in the ghetto: "He is doing the real harm to the Jews, because he doesn't have to make his money from these people and spoil their neighborhoods."

Mailer had once again chosen the Christians over the cannibals. But martyrdom goes unrewarded where voters are concerned. If the reverse was true, Daniel would have been delivered rather than devoured.

That afternoon, we took the candidates' traditional walk through the lower East Side and ate our fill at Ratner's dairy restaurant. But despite prodigious eating and the presence of Mailer's mother, who speaks Yiddish, we were subtly damned with *goyishe* civility instead of being blessed by Jewish love. Eighty percent of the questions had to do with our stand on CCNY. Didn't we know we were tearing down standards? Why should *they* get a free education without credentials? Sadly, one realized that no matter how liberal the community, one had only to dig deep enough and he would find a nigger in the woodpile of our national psyche.

Obviously, we had made one political blunder too many. A poll released by CBS Television stated that 88 percent of the city's people were against open admissions. But it was a disaster of our own making, one in which we collectively believed and wouldn't have deserted.

So like those stalwarts on the *Titanic*, we held hands and went down singing.

5
The Sorrowful Mysteries on the Way to the Mountaintop

A CURIOUS thing was taking place. The mirror in which the electorate found the candidate that fit their individual images now was fragmented between the four other candidates. (Seder had withdrawn in favor of Badillo.) Mailer couldn't claim a sliver for his own, and our campaign was rendered faceless.

Strangely, a Wagner poll showed that we were not without some body. According to his pollster, we were holding 12 percent of the vote, or 100,000 voters. But these voters were no distinguishable part of the whole by party, by income, or by ethnic background. They were the dust on the fringes of the fragmentation, the far-flung from all sides who formed an unreflective constellation. Mailer was an adhesive to the scattered.

The reasons for this could be found in Mailer's charming personal unorthodoxy and in his ideas. Our position papers had begun to garner attention around the city. Ferris had delivered a brilliant paper on housing that provided for taking the $16,000,000 the city currently spends on demolition of old buildings and funding Neighborhood Housing Banks. The banks would lend out this same amount to local residents who wanted to reclaim these buildings and renovate them. The paper also stated that pressure would be put on established banks in neighborhoods to subsidize these new banks by lending money for purchase or improvement of housing at the lowest interest rate possible, thus forcing the banks to serve their immediate communities. The renovation would be accomplished by local residents under professional supervision with funds derived from a funded Manpower Training Program. It was a classic example of the Ferris theory that government can come home again.

Cliff Adelman and Manso produced an education paper which carried the concept of local school control further than any other candidate. Locally elected school boards would be given the right to hire and fire their own teachers and to negotiate separate union contracts with teachers in each neighborhood. Teachers could strike against their own neighborhood school board, but by agreement they could not go out in sympathy with teachers in other neighborhoods. This plan would avoid an all-out strike of the sort that had crippled all the city's schools in 1968. Needy neighborhoods also could use paraprofessionals to teach in their schools, and more innovative neighborhoods could construct vest-pocket campuses in private housing, freeing themselves from the whims of the Board of Estimate and the wheezing pace of the construction unions.

Of course, there were the constant throwaway ideas from the candidate and the staff, affecting various layers of depth but consistent in their affection for urban life: make Coney Island a Las Vegas East; free bicycles in all city parks; cable TV to be controlled by neighborhoods; a central farmers' market offering ethnic foods of all varieties; a zoo in every neighborhood; a World Series of stickball to be held in the deserted Wall Street district on weekends; offering various incentives to encourage policemen to live in the precinct in which they work; a United States Grand Prix in Central Park yearly; and the recognition of Muhammad Ali as heavyweight champion of the world. The author of the last needs no identification.

Granted, it was not an intellectual banquet, but in a campaign without marrow it was a stew that found some spare ribs to stick to. The idea that really caught fire was the construction of a monorail around the island of Manhattan with attaching spurs originating in the boroughs. In each there would be a giant municipal parking lot at the boarding sites, and the whole system would be augmented in the Manhattan midtown area by electric jitney buses that would move uptown and across town between 32d and 59th streets and First and Ninth avenues. The jitneys would be similar to cable cars with running boards and open sides. In bad weather accordion side flaps would be closed. The jitney concept was derived from a similar idea of city planner Mary Hommann and expanded and altered by Mailer and Manso. The monorail was a love child of Mailer's. I watched him work over the project in his apartment, as Ray Geller provided the sketches. He estimated costs per mile ($5,000,000 against the city's figure of $37,500,000 for subways), the size and weight of the cars, and the speed at which they could travel safely without crumbling the structure that would support them. He threw figures around like New York's old master builder, Bob Moses. I viewed these proceedings intrigued but skeptical—was he trying for the Pulitzer Prize for Fiction, indeed Science Fiction?

When I suggested that his computations would be open to challenge, Mailer airily informed me that he had studied engineering at Harvard. And when he released his paper, his figures held up. The New York *Post* consulted an expert on transportation who found the concept, in terms of both construction and finance, totally feasible. Congressman Ed Koch of New York's 19th C.D. read the paper into the *Congressional Record*. The press labeled it the Mailer Rail, and editorial columnists urged further investigation of the project. It was a gift from the gods that I hadn't expected—a mathematician who was mean with a metaphor.

Even the money situation improved. Fifteen thousand dollars

was channeled into the campaign: nine of it for a book* that was to be a complete collection of our position papers and postmortems by the staff, and six for a film that was to be shot by Dick Fontaine of the BBC, who previously had filmed Mailer's famous march on the Pentagon.

And Steinem, in California working on a book about Cesar Chavez, constantly kept in touch by supplying lovely gold diggers to arrange parties and fund raisers. Two of these ladies, Joyce Mitchell and Pat Luce, worked to supply name talent for our various bashes; while their partners, Bonnie Lewis and Linda Francke, scouted the city for discothéques and living rooms to house the affairs. They were a hardworking foursome; but through his perverse obstinacy and whims, Mailer was to prove a hard sell, and this once merry quartet soon began to sound like a Greek chorus.

Lee Cook remained a source of irritation and embarrassment to me. It was late in the campaign, and we had done only minimal campaigning in the Black communities, a natural turf for our platform of local control. Cook continually advised that the time was not yet ripe, that he was working with the Black leaders to pave the way for our triumphant entrance. These "leaders'" leadership seemed to be the best-kept secret in the communities. But endless clandestine meetings always were in the making behind one closed door or another. It became evident to me that "circle jerking" was not an exclusive province of the liberals.

Besides, sometimes after weeks of absence, Cook would show up at headquarters to collect his paycheck, one promised him by Mailer. It was an arrangement that did not sit well with many of the full-time volunteers who could have used a little money for their time and work in place of my constant poor-mouthing, particularly when Cook's supposed liaison did not

---

* *Running Against the Machine*, Doubleday, 1969.

open any doors in the Black communities to us. It was a difficult problem with which to deal, since Mailer seemed taken with Cook's mystique. And it was not only Mailer. Other leftists in our camp who could be vehement about the CIA seemed to have a secret closet of the heart that housed a cloak and dagger.

In the end, it was the reliable Ferris who penetrated the ebony curtain. He called some residents of Bed Stuy whom he had helped form block associations and plant trees. Once the deed was accomplished, Mailer forgot about all the previous machinations and declared: "That Ferris is terrific." And when Mailer began to walk the streets of the Brooklyn slum, all my previous annoyance disappeared. He was a white man who came to listen and not to talk. Small groups would engage him for twenty minutes at a time, citing their grievances. And when I would prod him to move on, so that he would get more "exposure," he rightfully and testily would explain that we had a lot to learn.

In addition, I put Dustin Smith in touch with a militant's nightmare, a Black matriarch in a flowered hat who was in Breslin's corner because of his community stand during the previous year's school strike; and a Harlem street rally went into formation.

Since the CCNY stand, Breslin also was in high spirits. The very idea that he had taken the side of the kids seemed once more to light his days with grace. And it was with the young that his actions were secure, whether those at headquarters or those on campus. The vaunted carouser was very much a father figure.

When they walked the streets, it was hardly noticeable that they were together. Breslin would be the lead scout fifty feet ahead of Mailer, stopping to perch a leg up on a stoop and ask a group of shipwrecked men at sea on wine: "What do you think of this bullshit? Does what we're saying make any sense to you?" Then his regular parting: "God bless."

Mailer was the philosophical trailer immersed in dialogue with Young Turks and aging street orators. Their reception was warm, as warm, one supposed, as any white man except Lindsay would receive. Jimmy's waddle would produce a bubbly giggle from the ladies as he approached them. Norman's jauntiness and respectful ear gained him the guarded accolade of the ghetto: "Hey, man, at least you had the balls to come."

When they walked the white neighborhoods, Breslin was legend and Mailer lover. Jimmy constantly was joshed about being out in the hot sun instead of in some watering hole. And if he was missing from the campaign trail, we used his reputation. When his absence was questioned, we would respond with a smirk that "he was working Queens." It was a response that produced guffaws that hinted of "I bet he is!" So if the real Breslin couldn't be found, the hint of a hangover produced votes among the sane and the cynical who know that men of quality don't expose themselves to the noonday sun.

Norman, though more esoteric, produced more excitement. The ladies were his: the young ones responding to his sensitivity and sexuality, the older ones—having too much sense to worry about the former—pursued the latter. Such a case was a Jewish woman on Flatbush Avenue who broke through the crowd crooning, as she pinched his cheek, "Hell-o there, sexy!" She was followed by another, who mingled erotica with reality, saying, "Darling, good luck. You'll need it," as she patted him.

And Mailer was the one who was capable of delivering private parcels of wit. A grave young man in Brooklyn told him he primarily liked his books, but he would vote for him anyway. Mailer, sizing up his man, gazed into his sincere face and said, "Thank you, sir. At least the bad news will be couched in elegant language."

Elegance aside, Breslin returned to the campaign in his inimitable style, casting the first stones at everyone. His renewed presence buoyed the staff and deflated the opposition. Even the distaff side wasn't spared. He said of Elinor Guggenheimer, a former city planner and his opposition for the City Council presidency on Badillo's ticket, that he hoped she was one of those Guggenheimers who dealt in public philanthropy, because when he was done with her, she would become a ward of the state. To the New York *Times*, he once again cited Wagner's contemporaneity by saying the ex-mayor kept abreast of events by reading the New York *Herald Tribune* (a paper that had died three years before). At a press conference, he awarded Mario Procaccino the "Marvin the Torch" Award, because in Breslin's opinion, Mario's election would promise a city in flames.

The hitherto mannerly Mailer's verbal guns also became more august. Badillo, to whom he had been gentle in the past, was not spared. In a television debate Mailer took the gloves off, declaring: "Badillo and the rest of the liberals haven't had a new idea in twenty-two years." It struck me that this was the third time Mailer had used the number twenty-two (at the Gate and in the Channel 11 and Channel 13 debates), and each time in a different context. Was Mailer saying something the electorate was not catching? Jimmy, never one to be covert, raised the ante on attacking Badillo: "Being the relocation commissioner under Wagner is like being the lookout on the *Titanic*."

It became increasingly apparent that Breslin's barrage was not a careless, shoot-from-the-hip attack, but a well-planned shelling to psych out his opponents for their upcoming TV debates. God, one marveled at his mastery. When the *Times* called him to be interviewed along with his opposition (five other Democrats and two Republicans), he told the paper: "I refuse to be interviewed for such a story. I am too big a man, after twenty years, to be lumped into a story with seven other office clerks." As usual, he was hinting at a truth.

Hugh Carey, Wagner's man, had had little exposure outside his native Brooklyn. Mrs. Guggenheimer, though a delicate teacup in Manhattan, obviously wouldn't hold much water with the mugs in Brooklyn and Queens. Charles Rangel, Scheuer's mate, was a state assemblyman from Harlem, and his color wasn't very big this season. Robert Low, an independent entry, was a city councilman from Manhattan, one of those twitchy reformers who looks ideal for a Compōz commercial and whose major contribution had been to stage a tennis match with a pro for the television cameras to demonstrate to the youth of the city that "one must play by the rules of the game." A move which brought forth from the young a double zero, or in tennis terms, No Love.

The unlikely heavyweight was Procaccino's running mate, Francis X. Smith, the current City Council president, who had ascended to the position when Frank O'Connor deserted to run unsuccessfully against Nelson Rockefeller for governor. Smith, like those bogus heavyweights who had tried to wear Cassius Clay's crown, looked at best pleasantly bewildered.

This innocuous field moved Lindsay's former deputy mayor, Bob Price, to say in the *Wall Street Journal* that Breslin's popular name might carry him to victory. Which moved Breslin to comment: "That son of a bitch is trying to scare the shit out of me." So the scene was set for a confrontation between a noted son of the sidewalks and five others who weren't exactly household names in the tradition of Groucho, Harpo, Chico, Zeppo, and Spiro.

The first battleground was to be NBC's Direct Line debate, sponsored by the League of Women Voters and hosted by Vic Roby. When I arrived, Breslin was going over the issues with Newfield, who exchanged strained but civil greetings with me. Then I accompanied Breslin to the makeup room. We went over the staff's prepared facts while Breslin was being beautified. A *Daily News* photographer took a shot of Breslin wincing under the blow of a powder puff, a photo they would prominently display in an article on Mailer and Breslin called "The Bore Busters." It was consistent with that paper's puckish style.

They had run a photo of Breslin on the day of his announcement drinking a glass of water at the podium, captioned: "Jimmy Breslin Oils His Tonsils."

Breslin was a balloon of nerves, puffing slim cigars and scrawling notes on a yellow legal pad in a big, circular, Palmer Penmanship script. Inside the studio before air time he was more relaxed, chatting with the other candidates. For all his gruff attacks on them, they seemed to like him, knowing that when he threw something at them, it was not a brickbat but a soft, creamy pie. Performers all, they couldn't help appreciating a good turn. All, that is, except the lady.

It was quite obvious that Breslin's Brueghelian charm was lost on her—Ellie was a connoisseur of Watteau. Of course, Breslin exacerbated the situation at every encounter. When she had snubbed him at an earlier political club meeting, he had cracked loudly to the gathering that her hostility came from the fact that she was "after his body." Mailer, it seemed, was erotically influencing our ex-altar boy.

The burning question of the debate was the CCNY settlement. Rangel was "in general" for the agreement but with many provisional "ifs" and "buts." Carey, Smith, Guggenheimer, and Low were firmly against. Breslin, of course, was pro, and as usual he added his infinite wisdom. He stated that the standard way to win a race in New York City was "to kick a Black, preferably a welfare mother, in the shins two weeks before election day." The moderator and the opposition gasped equally at his blackprint for victory, and he succeeded in baiting them into attacking instead of cleverly ignoring him.

Mrs. Guggenheimer found his notion of a fifty-first state "absurd" and countered with her concept of "regionalism," a plan that would join New Jersey, Connecticut, and New York together in fighting such problems as air and water pollution. It was a gross blunder. If statehood was an absurdity to the average voter, at least it smacked of autonomy; but the idea of a New York-New Jersey-Connecticut troika was downright ludicrous.

Carey and Smith, the favorites, tried to concentrate their attacks on each other but mistakenly allocated too much time to rebutting Breslin. Rangel, because of Jimmy's stand with the minorities, was forced to deal with him most lovingly. Low hysterically attacked everyone, flaunting his purity as an independent candidate. It was a dubious ploy to offer a town that genuflects to "connections."

Breslin insisted that the ghetto youth were ready for college in a unique way, because when it came to "sight and sound, no other group is more attuned to the sixties." When he talked of neighborhood control, he cited the neighborhoods by the parish churches and synagogues that define their borders. During this colloquy Carey sat enthralled, and one surmised he was cribbing notes for future campaigning. In a move to mock Low's claim to independence, Breslin told the story of a former Mayor O'Brien who had run on a platform that "he was unbossed." According to Breslin, the unbossed O'Brien was asked on his inauguration day whom he was going to appoint as his police commissioner and he answered: "I don't know. They haven't told me yet."

Curiously, the best debate took place off camera between Breslin and Breslin. While another candidate was speaking, Breslin furiously scribbled in his notebook or talked to himself, complete with oratorical gestures and grimaces. He was so involved in this inner debate that he was oblivious to all signals from Newfield and me to stop it. On he went, poking the air with a pertinent finger, mouthing and scowling silent denunciations, then triumphantly sitting back and grinning at a quartered foe. Our concern, of course, was that the camera would focus on one of these sessions, and tomorrow legend would have it: "Jesus, you should have seen it. Breslin was drunk."

At the end, Carey seemed to have come across as the most competent, though surprisingly Francis X. had displayed some of that naïve "Mr. Smith Goes to Washington" charm and run a close second. Breslin was placed among the top three in varying degrees by our staff consensus with his most moving moment being a plea for youth: "We are spilling our treasure across the floors of the Criminal Courts Building."

But Breslin didn't buy our rating, and he immediately went to the phone to call Rosemary. He emerged from the booth saddened. The true index of his behavior had rendered her verdict. "I don't know if it's because she's so goddamned against this thing or not," Breslin said, "but she told me I finished dead last."

Unlike the famous Kennedy-Nixon debates, these municipal confrontations held no dramatic impact, and it was difficult to gauge who gained what. Because of the intense anti-Lindsay feeling in the city, the race for City Council had become a nonentity and was eclipsed by the mayoralty contest. The Democrats, riding Lindsay's back and with their huge registration edge, felt anyone they produced (except an unlikely Mailer) could win. So for the most part the debates weren't oriented toward distinguishing individuals, but to a collective display of antidotes, each capable of purging Lindsay. The result was that one was left only with impressions.

Mailer's best moment came in the last debate, when Wagner proclaimed he had been instrumental in bringing Scheuer, Badillo, and Procaccino into public life, to which Mailer retorted: "Now you finally have handcuffed all of you together where you belong." And in the same meeting, as Mailer eloquently summed up the need for a fifty-first state, Vic Roby, the moderator, entranced, said: "Thank you, Governor."

In sum, there was Wagner's wise "I've been here before" and Badillo's brisk efficiency. Scheuer throughout remained a decent intruder and Procaccino a buffoon, but a clown who sang the same teary refrain of how only *he* had stood up to *them* and reopened City College. Procaccino was not a performer who would win cheers in an open, lighted tent where one's applause signifies allegiance. But the voting booth is no bright big top. It is a dark confessional with a curtain to muffle the blackest intents of the soul.

Banning had become the most visible member of the campaign staff. He and Mailer were inseparable. It was a relationship that worried Tully and me, because we felt Banning's allegiance to the candidate would cloud his reports on how Mailer was really doing on the stump. But it was a situation with which we had to live, since whenever we had assigned anyone else to travel with Mailer, the accounts of the day sounded like the magical mystery tour. I would be besieged with requests for "one more appearance in Queens to put us over the top." Romantics we had enough of, and Banning—friendship aside—at least tempered his reports with reality. He saw himself as too much of a pro to do otherwise.

Mailer continued to rant against "beards and leftists" and still felt his campaign hadn't reached the "real people." Some of his bitching was justified. Staff cars would appear bearing crudely lettered signs that gave the campaign the appearance of a psychedelic crusade. And an unknown flake in the Bronx even toured the borough one day with a truck emblazoned with the message UP AGAINST THE WALL, MOTHERFUCKER. A position—on paper or otherwise—we hadn't as yet adopted.

But for the most part the "beards and leftists" who rallied to our banner were the foundation of the campaign. Without them, we had nothing. Indeed, we wouldn't even have had a place on the ballot. Mailer's carping would have been tolerable if he had chosen to deal with specifics rather than generalities. Besides, his own conduct and many of his further-out stands (hippies making love on the tops of cars in their own neighborhoods, Sweet Sunday) were more antagonistic to the working class than the sight of a collection of beards. If he wanted to play it one way, fine. But I didn't accept his schizophrenic vision of the campaign. After all, these "freaks," not the white working class, had moved an uncaring nation to question their racism and an immoral war. For the first time, I began to feel "No More Bullshit" was so much bullshit.

But the pace of a campaign murders reflection. The plotting of strategies is steamrolled under by the day-to-day action. Dustin Smith and Paul Schwartzman organized a rally on the steps of the Federal Building on Wall Street at noon. From the size of the crowd (newspapermen present estimated 2,000), they had done their job well.

But one can't figure the enthusiasm of a Wall Street lunch-hour crowd, since their boredom quotient is high. Forced to eat lunch in those grind-them-out-tuna-on-rye factories, the workers usually end up with forty-five minutes to kill after they have eaten. This is the same crowd that gathers by the hundreds to hear sidewalk preachers advocate everything from sexual abstinence to the burning of the Stock Exchange. Did our magnetism draw them, or were we just another interlude to help them digest their Chicken of the Sea?

When we arrived, a quartet obtained by the coordinators was playing chamber music to attract the crowd. Mailer promptly pronounced them the equal of a "fuckin' Salvation Army Band." Since we argued about everything these days, I bit my lip and passed up a dissertation on music appreciation. Besides, I was growing tired of having Mailer tell me I had "a thick fuckin' Irish skull," a criticism that many times was solid as a rock.

Jimmy warmed them up with some charming light stuff about

his association with such dubious financiers as loan sharks. And Norman, sizing up the terrain, dwelt on the financial benefits of the fifty-first state. Their performance was received cordially, and when they mingled with the crowds there was some earnest questioning along with the backslapping. And as we headed for the car, one had to smile at the sight of a couple of Dreyfus lions, those guardians of capitalism, wearing the legend on their lapels: I WOULD SLEEP BETTER IF NORMAN MAILER WAS MAYOR.

An unexpected bonus presented itself. Gene Spagnoli, a reporter from the *Daily News*, that Bible of the Babbitts, asked to ride in the candidates' car for an interview. Here it was—Mailer's opportunity to reach the "real people" in a paper that finds its way into millions of "real homes" daily. A chance to lay out his program for neighborhood control for all neighborhoods, regardless of political persuasion. I began to have visions of an endorsement from the John Birch Society.

Immediately, I ordered three campaign workers out of the car to make room for Spagnoli and me. With all the subtlety of a Sennett actor attempting Feydeau, I winked repeatedly at Mailer and Breslin and said: "Spagnoli from the *News*, the DAILY NEWS." But gentle farceur that I am, I proved too subtle.

As we drove uptown, I waited for sounds of the blueprint of our white working-class utopia. Nothing. It was my turn to blow a big one by osmosis. I instructed the driver to drop me at headquarters, where I was to sit in on a meeting to discuss an upcoming fund raiser at the Electric Circus, a discothèque in the Village. It was to be a dinner at $25 a head with an open party afterward at $5 per. Linda Francke and her chorus had been working on the project for weeks, recruiting talent, printing invitations, and ordering food. The Circus already had given us space to store literature and house volunteers and now had offered their premises free for this occasion. Mailer had been fully aware of the project for three weeks, and we hoped to raise a minimum of $10,000 for some television time during the closing days of the campaign. But my man was never without surprises.

When he heard my instructions to the driver, he exploded: "We've had enough of this Greenwich Village shit! I hate that place. I spoke there three weeks ago. Did you ever see it? That place is warmed-over cancer." For the first time during the trip, Spagnoli was taking notes. Breslin chimed in to create "The Norm and Jimmy Show." He blustered that the next time he was in the Village, he'd personally kick the shit out of any hecklers. Spagnoli was still scribbling. Norman provided the capper: "Cancel the whole thing. We'll get money somewhere else." "Where?" I meekly tried, as the car whooshed away from headquarters.

The next day, Spagnoli recorded the Dynamic Duo, without a single reference to our "hip left-right coalition." The Circus was incensed. Linda Francke, who was about seven months pregnant, quit in shock, clutching her formidable stomach. It was an amazing campaign. Even the constituents of the womb weren't safe from it.

The following morning, I received a call from a female friend of Mailer's advising me that on Norman's orders I was to issue a statement supporting Beatle John Lennon's fight to obtain a United States visa. Lennon was in Canada, denied entry to the U.S. because of a pending marijuana charge. Incredulous, I asked her to repeat that this was Mailer's order, and she confirmed it. The same Mailer who the day before had wrecked the Circus affair, because the working class would think we were nothing but a bunch of Greenwich Village phonies. I hung up in disbelief. On this new day, the campaign was to champion a pot-smoking Limey Christ figure. Now there was a stroke that would endear us to the Irish workers out in Brooklyn and Queens.

Memorial Day we got lucky. Since Mailer wanted to meet the

people, Breslin and I planned a deliverance at Aqueduct Racetrack. Crowds on this holiday usually range near 70,000, the main attraction being the Metropolitan Handicap, a one-mile race. This year the favorite was Rokeby Stable's brilliant three-year-old, Arts and Letters. Such an omen was not lost on Mailer the Magician.

I already had a flyer made up to circulate among the devotees to the betterment of the breed, but the day before, Mailer (who previously had approved it) and the staff rejected it as too strong. The flyer had a picture of a fatigued Wagner and one of a sly, smiling Procaccino side by side with the caption, "If either of these guys win, they won't pass the urinalysis." At the bottom there was the usual exhortation to vote for Mailer-Breslin on June 17. I argued valiantly for my handiwork, but I was voted down. The staff felt that the press would crucify us for such irreverance. My losing argument was that the *Times* would be baffled about how to handle such delicate prose.

So with the aid of some inspirational Irish whiskey, the staff and I were induced to come up with a new entry about twelve hours before post time. On the wings of the whiskey, it became a labor of love. For the first time in weeks, the staff loosened up and laughed and griped in a fashion that is peculiar to combat units. The accidental evening proved to be an adhesive, binding us together for the run down the homestretch.

The project was my special province, because of my love for the racetrack, a love so profound that I probably would make my home in a stall if bestiality was socially acceptable. After many hours and multiple drinks, my final composition read thus:

We ran off the flyer on the mimeo machine and called it a night, only to find we had been locked in by the building superintendent and our only exit was the fire escape, one of the collapsible variety—hardly a garden path for such unnimble travelers to follow. But down we came, ever so slowly, until

AQUEDUCT

RAILBIRD'S PICKS

THE MAYORAL HANDICAP

June 17, 1969

P.P.	Horse	Comment	Pr. Odds
1	**WAGNER** 12-yr.-old gelding By Meade Esposito—Out of Machine	Knows the track.	8–5
2	**PROCACCINO** Bronx Ridgling By Fear—Out of Law and Order	Moves up on sloppy track.	2–1
3	**SCHEUER** By Liberal—Out of Loser	Can't tell them apart.	
3A	**BADILLO** By Liberal—Out of Loser		11–1
4	**MAILER ***BEST BET**** By Amateur—Out of Statehood	First-time starter. Good Barn.	20–1

TAKE A SHOT

MAILER-BRESLIN AND THE 51ST STATE AND MAILER-BRESLIN

Democratic Primary—June 17

under our collective weight the fire escape collapsed more swiftly than anticipated, depositing us on the sidewalk with a thud. It was an event of social significance: the first time since the St. Valentine's Day Massacre that a man vying for city rule nearly lost his mob in one clean sweep.

At the track Norman and Jimmy were a perfect parlay: Mailer in a blue blazer, his head a full-blown mast of curls, looked like the gentleman plunger; Breslin in a shocking pink shirt and a tablecloth of a tie (both in breadth and in its spackled colors) was out of the chorus of *Guys and Dolls*. A radiant Beverly Mailer added a big plus on the distaff side.

The crowd in its holiday mood gave us one of our best responses of the campaign. My tout sheet—in the perverse way of the press—became the darling of the day. The invaluable six o'clock news ran a clip of Mailer reading the entire handicap; the New York *Times* ran a photo story with a reprint of the sheet, burying Herman Badillo's "disclosure" of New York City's "hidden Vietnam budget." Street crowds a week later still were referring to it, and even the pantheon of the press, *Time* magazine, mentioned it. In retrospect it was my biggest contribution to the campaign.

The next day I talked to Mailer on the phone, and he was elated—not only by our reception with the crowd and the press, but he'd also had a good day at the betting windows. He had placed $90 on Arts and Letters, who scored a come-from-behind victory. Moreover, to him, Arts and Letters had overcome a symbolic handicap. "When I saw him coming through the stretch," Mailer said, "I said to myself, 'Maybe, maybe.' "

But elation is not always a good thing in a candidate. Candidates have the tendency to see themselves as the sole architects of their good fortune and tend to ignore the advice of others and lose their discipline. Mailer was no exception. Indeed, because of the swath of his personality, he was more vulnerable than most. It was at this point, with less than two weeks to go, that he started to manage or, more precisely, dictate his own campaign.

When we began our run, we agreed that as a matter of policy we would not give our endorsement to any other candidate for office. Mailer, now riding high, chose the closing period of our campaign to break this promise. Laird Cummings invited Mailer to address his political club on Manhattan's upper West Side. Bentley Kassal, a club member and a candidate for district civil court, approached Mailer and asked him for an endorsement before the club. Mailer, impressed with his newfound political prominence, did so—knowing nothing about Kassal's politics.

It was a move that infuriated the staff, since we had no desire to add our presence to the incestuous bed of West Side politics. But Cummings was the one who really was burned, since he so opposed Kassal's politics he had run against him in the past. He asked Mailer to withdraw the endorsement, the candidate refused, and Cummings quit as campaign coordinator.

Other heady Mailer moves were to come. Steinem, back in town, raised additional cash, and we decided to use it for an ad in the Week in Review section of the Sunday New York *Times*, the most politically potent showcase in the city. The staff argued for a "clean" ad with plenty of white space, outlining our main positions and prominently displaying the candidates' names.

Mailer insisted on using the space to write an open letter to the voting Democrats of the city. He was to have his way—an open letter it would be. He promised to keep it relatively short and to the point, so it could be set in readable type. And when we rejected the idea of tacking on the bulk of our platform at the letter's conclusion, he agreed. But this was Tuesday. I learned something about Norman's promises—Never on Sunday.

When the ad appeared, 90 percent of our own workers missed it, even though they were expecting it. The letter was printed in type that was last used in the Japanese code. In fact, the type was so small that it probably was the first political ad in the *Times*' history it didn't have to microfilm. Besides, the letter contained another attack on the press that made us sound like we were whining and concluded with an inane slogan that a resident of Bedford Stuyvesant had given Mailer, which he took to his heart as a cobblestone of street genius. To wit: "... a Black, middle-aged man with a round head, round belly and a big smile. He shook our hand. 'We've had the rest,' he said, 'Now try the best. Vote Mailer-Breslin.' "

To boot, Mailer went back on his word and added a couple of thousand words on six of our platform planks in type infinitely smaller than the letter! Pete Hamill remarked that he had missed the ad, because he thought it was a statement of bankruptcy. To me, the layout was similar to those advertisements in *Silver Screen* magazine that promised to cure your acne if you mailed the coupon below to a box number in Cincinnati.

Only Heidi Tully had a kind word for Mailer's ad. She commented that it might find readers among those Sunday morning ritualists who leisurely read the *Times* while sitting on the john. Her less romantic husband, Paul, retorted: "Yeah, you might be in there long enough to finish it if you were dying from dysentery." The whole fantastic farrago cost us $4,000.

But like the Sorrowful Mysteries of the Rosary, our sad string had not yet run out. Once, explaining my managerial role to Mailer, I had used a boxing allusion—saying that my job was to get all of us through fifteen rounds with the best part of us still intact. Since I well realized we were a collection of florid egos, I knew there would be scars and bruises but none so deep, I hoped, that in the end we couldn't sit down, bathe them in booze, and laugh at the whole damn thing. So far, I had been able to achieve just that, even through the harmful Newfield affair. Jack and I knew the depth of our antagonism and now were back conversing and enjoying a social drink together. Besides, he'd also managed to get a parting shot into print: "This [speaking of his being fired] is like being banned from Auschwitz."

But my cherished manipulation came to an end. On June 5, Mailer managed (with a big assist from Banning) to put poison into the campaign.

Much in the manner of every candidate through history, Mailer started to purge his ranks. He wanted visible proof of his troops' "loyalty." And "loyalty" in these waning days seemed to mean subservience. If one argued tactics with the candidate, he was flirting with treason. This is a very human reaction among candidates—especially one who has a strong chance of losing. Because, when the results come in, he's the one who stands alone. If everything comes up roses, the winner will bear his garland proudly. But who among men does not want to share a crown of thorns? And on election eve, Cronkite and Huntley-Brinkley on their election boards would not record our collective boobery, but would praise Mailer for his flocking legion or, more likely, indict him for his dismal body count.

So though I understood and was sympathetic to Mailer's machinations, I had other considerations. Or in the lexicon of his beloved gutter: "I can feel for you, baby, but not reach you."

Mailer had his unquestioned loyalty from his constant companion, Bill Walker, and lately also from Luke Breit, a young poet and the son of writer Harvey Breit, who had joined him and Walker on the daily rounds. But they were only on the fringe of the campaign, and Mailer wanted to probe deeper. He chose Banning as a symbol to castrate the leftists who haunted him. He got him to shave off his beard. One could question the political significance of a hank of hair, but then that same one forgets—contrary to myth, campaigns are composed of men, not issues. And Mailer demeaned Banning as a man.

When Banning's woman, Sandra, confronted her plucked lover that day on the street, she cried and vehemently cursed both him and Mailer. An overreaction, one might surmise in the general scheme of things. But who is to know in the more profound scheme of the sheets what delights that tuft rendered the lady? Moreover, to shave it off unbeknownst to her at the request of another man! Mailer, who had bridled at what he interpreted as an attack on his manhood by James Wechsler, should have known better than to issue a request that smacked of punk. The lady's curses were divinely delivered. Who can comprehend the shock she felt that evening when her cheek sought out that familiar, warm ball of yarn, only to find a foreign, cold darning egg?

When I and other members of the staff confronted the "new" Banning, we didn't help to soothe matters. Cruelly, we made him an object of derision. I told him his chin looked like a show girl's shaven cunt, and the others were just as unkind. But more cruelly, Mailer pompously defended Banning as "loyal," the only one who had made "a sacrifice" for a chance at a victorious campaign. Then Mailer, taking a swipe at my whiskers (though I thought he was aiming lower), informed me that I had to remain off the campaign trail during the closing days. He began introducing Banning as his co-campaign manager. Neither move drove me to lather.

Mailer's pats on Banning's head did not achieve their desired effect. Indeed, the opposite occurred. Banning saw the ludicrous role in which Mailer had cast him, a role that reached its apex on a day in Coney Island when we were to ride the Cyclone (Coney's famed roller coaster) as a campaign publicity gimmick. Mailer told me not to ride in the car with him because "every newspaper picture will have your fuckin' beard in it" and summoned Banning to his side.

When Bill Walker, whom Banning saw as a political albatross to the campaign, shaved off his beard to prove his undying "loyalty," Banning was racked with self-disgust. He now was running in company he disdained. Thus, such an unlikely incident provoked a division in the campaign that in the favorite phrase of candidate Mario Procaccino produced "good guys and bad guys."

Banning's bitterness ran deep, and his effectiveness slipped immeasurably. His open hostility to Mailer began to manifest itself in public places. With twelve days to go, Mailer had committed an incredible blunder. When he needed Banning most, through some perverse need in his own ego he deliberately diminished the most valuable member of his campaign staff. For all the time they had spent together, Mailer learned little of Banning. It wasn't the loss of the beard, or his woman's scorn, or the unkind taunts about his surrender that really mattered. Mailer stole what he cherished most. With one emotionally bush league act, Banning surrendered his sacred standing among the chilly pros.

It now was apparent to our staff and key workers that the campaign had broken in two: the one I directed from headquarters and the one Mailer and his "loyalists" conducted from his home in Brooklyn Heights. My phone calls to the candidate were screened by Walker, who constantly put me off with the whispered admonishment "Norman is sleeping." A line which at headquarters was transformed bitchily into "Ah-h, Norman's taking a nappy-poo."

I was at a loss to stop the festering, and our private bile started to run over in public. At a block party in Brooklyn, Banning, who was boozing, insulted Mailer and nearly prompted a fight between himself and Walker. On another day Mailer, Banning, and I were joined by New York *Times*' columnist Tom Wicker on the campaign trail. We took the traditional ride on the Staten Island Ferry to campaign among that borough's commuting workers. Staten Island was the heartland of John Marchi and conservatism, and as we walked the ferry handing out our literature and shaking hands, I tried to estimate how many pleasant breakfasts were churning in tune with the ferryboat.

After the ride we campaigned at subway stops in Brooklyn, and Banning, manning the sound system in the car, insidiously started to dig Mailer. In a pandering voice he announced: "Yessir, ladies and gentlemen, step up and meet Norman Mailer. It's really him! The Pulitzer Prize winner and author of that brilliant first novel *The Naked and the Dead*. Step right up, folks—it's really him! In person!" Wicker happily construed the invective as good-natured joshing and wrote a highly favorable column, stating: "At best, they [the other candidates] are offering more or less of the same, while Mailer argues that it is impossible 'to change the city for the better without creating a new political basis.' " He then surmised: "What Mailer and Breslin have done is to dramatize a fundamental issue, not only for New York but for all America, in demanding 'a new beginning.' "

It was the third consecutive laudatory column we had received on the *Times*' editorial page. (Columnist Russell Baker and editorial writer John A. Hamilton penned the others.) So even though our dirty linen was flapping in public, it had not yet been aired in print.

But Banning proved resilient and rose again from the dead. Not for the lofty reasons one attributes to the originator of that particular hat trick, but for a chance to shine in his beloved media. We had raised another $4,000 to buy spot commercials on radio, and Banning had visions of his golden tones seducing the electorate to our cause. But the newly risen Banning was to suffer a spiritual phenomenon—a double crucifixion.

The headquarters staff (Tully, Banning, and I) gathered at Linda Francke's home, along with Joanne Pickett, who had done radio commercials for Robert Kennedy, to write our material. After hours of haggling, we managed to compose seven thirty-second spots for the candidates to choose from. Tully's darkly humorous, surefire winner—a Jewish woman screaming, "My purse!" followed by the sounds of machine-gun fire and a Negro's whining voice saying, "You got me," followed by Banning's best Moses voice tagging off, "Vote Mailer-Breslin for Real Law and Order"—was rejected roundly by all, but not for its analytical brilliance.

We scheduled the taping for June 11 and submitted the spots we'd written to Mailer. He read our efforts, but there was no word of praise or damnation heard at headquarters. So as Banning, Tully, Francke (whom we induced back for "a female voice" and the promise of a good farewell party), Manso, Joyce Mitchell, and I waited in the sound studio on West 44th Street, we had no idea what we were going to record. Like Beckett characters not knowing their next move, we were waiting for Mailer.

Joanne Pickett and her husband, Bob, a radio announcer, arrived with the sound engineers, and the small studio became as crowded as an unfaithful wife's closet. To make matters worse, Dick Fontaine arrived with his film crew to shoot the event for posterity. So what little air was left was being cooked by the movie lights. To alleviate the situation, I sent out for a couple of cases of beer, a brilliant tactic which saved our brains from baking but not from steaming.

Mailer finally came in and promptly told us that our collective craftsmanship was "a lot of shit." Blunt, to be sure, but one genuflects to his literary betters, and we awaited his brilliant thirty seconds. By this time, I had forgiven his *Times*' opus, figuring that the gray old lady of journalism just didn't sex up the candidate enough. But now he had the electronic airways to charge his genius, and we were anxious. He inexplicably stalled.

For good reason. When he revealed what we were to record, the room exploded. He had written an honest-to-God jingle! It was based on the street nugget he had picked up in Bedford Stuyvesant: "You Had the Rest—Now Vote the Best," with thirty seconds of Paris saloon circa 1920 repetitions. If the collective mentality of the electorate was that of Alice B. Toklas, we were home an easy winner.

I screamed, telling him he had gone too far this time. Tully pleaded with him as a football coach pleads with a gifted but loony quarterback. Breslin burst into the studio, took one look at the script, and bellowed: "Bullshit, we have too much class for this." Banning walked to the microphone and in announcers' tones said: "Welcome to the Mailer-Breslin Circle Jerk Studio." Joanne Pickett moaned: "My God, my Bob isn't going to read that; he's a professional." I sent out for another case of beer.

Mailer started to brood under our attack. In his own mind, we once again were all against him. He told Breslin to read the jingle aloud, and it would sound good in his ear. Jimmy countered: "You could have Richard Burton read it, and it don't do nothin' to my ear." I went back at Mailer and told him it was impossible. He shouted: "I'm sick and fucking tired of arguing with you. We'll do it my way. It's my money." Banning pleaded again on the basis of his professional radio experience, but Mailer shouted him down, too. Banning slumped in his chair, his arms outstretched, his hands and the last vestige of his professionalism waiting for the nails.

As the man said, it was his money, so we prepared to record. Breslin and I were chosen to read the commercial, presumably because we sounded like the only legitimate members of the Dead End Kids in the campaign. What followed had to be more traumatic to the ghost of Ed Murrow than the Battle of Britain was to his person. For fourteen takes, Breslin and I, alternating roles (one monotonously reading the opposition's names, the other snappily giving the jingle), read the following:

Wagner–Badillo–Scheuer–Procaccino–Esposito,
Wagner–Esposito–Badillo–Wagner–Wagner,
Wagner–Wagner.

You had the rest,
Now vote the best,
Mailer-Breslin, fifty-one.
Mailer-Breslin and the fifty-first state,
Vote Mailer-Breslin and the fifty-first state.
Democratic primary. Tuesday.

Takes were interrupted by Jimmy's stopping and shouting: "I don't like the copy after the four Wagners. It's got fuckin' cancer." Or: "Jesus, Norman, it sounds like an Excedrin commercial." Or such coaching gems to me as: "Joe, the beer is bad for your breathing"; or Banning shouting at me: "You prick, you stole my beer!" Orson Welles would have been impressed.

After many, many beers, Jimmy decided that one take (because of our accents) had a Jersey City charm like: "Vote for Jimmy McHugh. He's a father, a Legionnaire, and Father Murphy from St. Dominick's recommends him." "The fuckin' thing," Breslin surmised, "will go over great in Hoboken." Banning by now was reciting a drunken litany: "It's awful, it's awful, it's awful." On reflection, Breslin became his acolyte: "It's so bad, it's so bad, it's so bad." Mailer consoled: "After you hear it six or seven times, you'll love it." And Banning rejoined: "I'd rather fucking lose it than love it."

Number fourteen was it. Mailer was sober and satisfied. The rest of us were drunk and disgusted. The following Sunday at noon, it was aired, and an irate woman called headquarters demanding to speak to the campaign manager. She accused me of embarrassing a great candidate with my asinine mind and said I should be fired for creating such a stupid, vulgar commercial. With no more patience left, I shouted into the mouthpiece: "Madame, believe it or not, you just experienced a fucking Pulitzer Prize jingle."

On the evening of the day we taped, we attended a $50-a-head fund raiser at the East Sixties home of a diet doctor who was a friend of Beverly's. It was a sour collection of men who gathered at the baronial digs. The house, with its huge Spanish tile halls and impressive guests (Shirley MacLaine, David Merrick, and King Peter of Yugoslavia—honest!), looked like a Fellini set. To add to the dago decadence, there was a gilded cage of an elevator, the sort usually associated with dotty ladies with homosexual siblings in Tennessee Williams' plays. Two rock bands blared in the halls. Men in ice-cream-white Good Humor suits which hid their mirthless black souls drank with women in plastic see-through dresses, their tits and navels on display like packaged meat, a phenomenon of the sixties—Saran-Wrapped Sexuality.

The staff drank. Drank darkly. Contrary to the mutterings of the denizens of Harry Hope's saloon, there always is life in booze, but tonight it was as twisted as the hump on Richard III's back.

And it was here that I despaired. So far, I had checked my drinking during the campaign to three occasions: the Irish night in Brooklyn, my daughter's birth, and our day at the racetrack, all happy and brief encounters. Tonight, I knew this time around wouldn't be happy or brief. The best part of me (as on past occasions of drinking) started to erode. At first a hint of swoon in the soul, then the beginnings of surrender, and I darkly wondered—would one day the final sinister *s* follow? The last thing I wanted to visit on the campaign was another "ism" of the twentieth century. Mailer was at no fault here. The air I polluted was that which encased my own tight little island.

Mailer, though sober, was caught up in the blackness of the setting. He had discovered that cancer was indeed a galloping disease which hadn't come to a halt in Greenwich Village. Banning and Mailer traded civilized insolence, and I like a mummy case diseased a six-foot section of a far wall. Mailer, in what in retrospect was kindness, jocularly walked up and hooked me in the head: "Boy, would you like to punch me in the mouth!" Perception my man always had. I laughed, and for a moment he managed to break my mood. It was the kindest shot he threw at me during the campaign.

Free booze or not, the setting was unendurable. The staff decided to split to the Lion's Head, a familiar saloon in the Village, and the candidate for an appointment. We stood on the street waiting for the campaign cars, when Mailer without explanation hailed a cab, jumped in alone, and left his splintered staff and his wife behind him. As we stood there like bad gumshoes waving down the approaching campaign cars in a "follow that cab" manner, Beverly crowned our blackest day: "If you're going to stand in the middle of the street," she shouted, "take off your campaign buttons."

The next day, headquarters looked like a ward for the lobotomized and the shell-shocked. Tables where coffee cups once stood were populated with beer cans. The drinking was not blatant or boisterous, and only the most perceptive eye could sense the despair that prompted it. It was not only Banning, Tully, Whit, and Dustin Smith, and I, but the kids. No one got drunk or even slurred a word. In fact, it still was a sober operation.

What was taking place was that a band of once merrymakers, with the proper maintenance injection of alcohol, was reduced to functioning. Effective to be sure, but performing without wit or passion. Our magic had turned to voodoo. Headquarters was an island of the damned, the rulers and the ruled a functioning body of zombies.

6
Our Nada

IT would be hard to think of any campaign, except Napoleon's last, that ended in such disaster. For two weeks, nearly every day was a losing one. We got it from all sides. Even Breslin wasn't spared.

At an appearance at Gaelic Park in the Bronx, where he was to be introduced between halves of an Irish hurling match, we were booed and catcalled off the field. Over the years, both Breslin and I had written many perverse valentines about our ancestors, and on this sunny day the Celts, with their well-oiled tonsils, reciprocated. "Scum!" they greeted us. Their hostility was so great they committed the ultimate sacrifice of leaving the bar and their drinks to line the fence along the playing field to insult us. "Will you look at that fat bum," they jeered at Breslin. "Somebody knock his brains out, if the poor bastard has any," a voice as melodic as a harp added. When we reached the reviewing stand, the master of ceremonies refused to introduce him. Breslin and I sheepishly made our way back across the field of green to the exit. We weren't even granted a graceful departure. At the sight of Breslin and me together, one son of the old sod, whose face was as big and as red as a weather balloon, shouted: "Go home, Breslin, and take your fuckin' girlfriend with you." When we reached our car, someone had punctured one of the tires. The symbolism was perfect. Flat tires were what our campaign was all about these days.

But the Irish were to be pardoned. We were men for all treasons these days. The Jewish-oriented New York *Post* took the next shot. The paper was doing a full-page story on each of the candidates, and we anxiously awaited our day. It would be our chance to woo away Badillo's and Scheuer's liberal vote.

One of the paper's female journalists, a shy, plain-looking woman, was assigned to us; and Norman made the tactical error of strategic sexual overkill. He wined, dined, and conversationally charmed the life out of the lady, hoping for a glowing column on his person and his campaign. But Mailer forgot the age-old adage of wooing—tipsy ladies and plain Janes have mirrors both in the mind and on the vanity that tell the truth, and they rightfully suspect the overly solicitous.

In a column that one could take as being "generally" favorable, she planted seeds of our destruction. Such offhand remarks by Mailer as: "Badillo is a fine man, but he's not enough of a philosopher or a monomaniac." And Mailer's favorite quote: "Once a philosopher—twice a pervert." "Maniac" and "pervert" stuck with the reader—hardly the attributes the electorate was seeking in a man who, they hoped, would heal their mad city.

The lady, unlike the candidate, really understood effective overkill as she capsuled part of Mailer's career: ". . . three failed marriages (his fourth is alive and well in Brooklyn Heights); experiments with grass; nightly benders; encounters with the law after stabbing a wife (an episode which, incidentally, cut short an earlier plan to run for Mayor eight years ago)." Her implications smacked of bitchery: his fourth wife was *alive* and *well*—luckily, one presumed, for the moment, until the madman decided to cut short this bid for the mayoralty with the blade. What made it more insidious was that the press was aware (and bandied about the gory details in newspapermen's bars) of the domestic woes of the other candidates, including in one case an incident similar to Mailer's that involved alcohol and a knife. But, of course, these were "valuable" politicians, and Mailer was merely a social visionary and a man who towered above their profession. What can be said for an estate and its members' respect for their daily work that gleefully sullies its prized sons and protects and pampers the enemy of the people, the politician?

Things at headquarters remained the same—efficient and lifeless. Mailer cut himself off from all save Walker, Breit, and Peter Manso. Physical contact between *us* and *them* was nil. Only Manso occasionally showed at headquarters, and I suspected he was there to spy, since after each of his visits, Mailer called to complain about "the drinking." Because of these calls, Manso became unwelcome at 59th Street, and one night his presence nearly provoked a fight.

Besides, possibly because of his "inside" position these days, Manso physically started to mimic Mailer. Both men are short, and during normal times the similarity would end there. But lately, we had noticed that Manso's hair had become unruly, his speech staccato, his left hand jabbing home such Maileresque phrases as "liberal cocksuckers" and "jerkoff leftists." These affectations caused our valuable researcher meanly to be dubbed Mini-Mailer.

But even our most dismal days had some moments of light. Whit Smith's impressive paper on the financial structure of the fifty-first state was warmly received; and the candidate, as he was wont to do, had a day which made me fantasize that if I could have sequestered the entire voting public inside the same auditorium on that particular day, the prize would have been ours.

The setting was the enemy's battlefield, the auditorium of the Time-Life Building. Mailer was to speak to those magazines' employees. Somewhere in bygone print, he had equated the malaise of the country with that of *Time* magazine—both suffered from "Luce morals." And it was probably just because he was in the den of the devil that he gave such a brilliant account of himself. He jousted with them from the beginning, labeling them "cynics, surrealists, and malcontents," and proceeded to answer their queries in astonishing depth. He concluded with a peroration (delivered strictly off the cuff) which, if I had had all our expenditures back, I would have taped and shown endlessly on television. It was that moving to me and finally (regardless of our antagonistic absurdities) convinced me that not only was Mailer better than the rest, but also that perhaps only a monomaniac and a pervert who had been there twice had the daring to spring our soul from a wall-less asylum. In retrospect, I would have let our campaign stand or fall on the words that follow:

"So the notion that we're running on, finally, is that everybody in this city suffers from the same disease that everyone in America suffers from—that we suffer from it doubly, triply, and in exaggerated form—which is, we do not have a proper sense of our own identity. So, we argue that statehood, the quality of statehood, once achieved, would perform several wonders for this city. Not because we would get more money, although I think we would, and I think that money would be terribly necessary, but because the citizens of this city would have embarked upon an adventure in voting for that statehood particularly since we're the candidates at the moment who embody that desire. So, to get to statehood at that point, they would have to vote for us, which means that they would be deserting their belief in expertise, because we run on one notion over and over again, which is that the experts have driven this city right into the ground. And we run on the notion, finally, that politics is philosophy and that one cannot begin to solve the problems of a city without engaging in philosophical arguments with oneself and with one's neighbor.

"And the particular small continuing event which gives me the most pleasure since I've been campaigning is I find that I can give my speeches at the level at which I wish to give them. I never try to talk down; I say what I wish to say to an audience, trying to pick up the mood of that audience, talking at my best to reach that audience; and I find that the philosophical density of the argument never bothers them one bit. I've talked to left-wing audiences, to right-wing audiences, to all sorts of audiences, and they all listen. The right-wing audiences listen even more carefully than the left-wing audiences, perhaps because our words are fresher to them. At any rate, the powerful notion in it, which I think is appealing to all people in degree, is that if each group of people, each interest, each force in this city can begin to think in terms of neighborhoods, then it can begin to think in terms of discovering whether its own ideas and one's own ideas have validity, have savor, give energy to others, give energy to oneself—or don't.

"The tragedy of this city and the tragedy of this country is that we all live in a situation where none of us know what the reality is, and we explore for it and we explore for it—we spend our lives exploring for it—and we never find an objective ground where we can begin to locate whether some pet idea of ours or some profound idea of ours is partially true or partially untrue.

"To talk about the situation, even briefly, people on the right wing feel that the Black people are lazy, spoiled, ungrateful, and incapable of managing their own society. Black people feel, I would guess, on the one hand that they have extraordinary possibilities and that they are great people. On the other hand, they have to feel that they can't possibly know, because they never had an opportunity to express that desire. So, if nothing else, Black communities working with their own power in their own neighborhoods could show to other neighborhoods one of two things, which is either that Black people were right about their potentiality for the future, or that they were wrong and that, finally, they are incapable of making those extraordinary steps. And so that even right-wing people would have, at the end of that time, the confidence of knowing that they were seriously right or seriously wrong about some extraordinary matter. In turn, right-wing neighborhoods would discover in living with their principles whether their principles were nourishing and could maintain a society against all of the nihilistic tides of the twentieth century, or whether, finally, their principles were not sufficiently flexible to meet the extraordinary quality of the age. And on top of that, we would have the marvelous, if somewhat comic, alternatives of considering all those magical LSD communities where you would have children living on LSD for five years. At the end of that time, they would either be creating castles, or they might be two-thirds dead of liver disease.

"The notion that we're running on, then, is that until we begin to know a little more about each other—not through the old-fashioned New Deal governmental methods of tolerance—but through the quality of human experience in societies, small societies and somewhat larger societies founded upon various principles—philosophical, spiritual, economic, geographical, territorial, historical, or whatever—we know nothing at all.

"And that's why I feel a certain optimism about this candidacy. Because what I think it offers to all the people of the city of New York is a chance to turn this city around and make it what it once was—the leader of the world.

"Thank you."

But, once again, the gods giveth and taketh away. We were to lose our most worked-on and advanced street rally through another's tragedy. We had set aside one of the last Fridays before the primary for a street rally on the corner of 125th Street and Seventh Avenue outside the legendary Theresa Hotel in

Harlem. We had spent nearly $1,000 for trucks and sound equipment and recruited the services of cast members of the Broadway musical *Hair* for entertainment. Dustin Smith and his staff had worked for weeks with residents of Harlem to put the rally together. It was a day to which Mailer and, more important, a dispirited staff were anxiously looking forward. On the day of the rally, a young Muslim, Francis 27X Smith, was shot to death in a Harlem hallway; and the community, in a dark mood, was in no spirit to welcome white politicians. We painfully canceled the whole affair.

But the lesson learned was that our inconvenience was trivial, for as the Black man has told us for years: "You don't know the troubles I've seen."

I suppose only the lack of days saved us further lunacy. When men go on any kind of binge, only the timekeeper saves them. But we were rough men to bring to our knees, and there were a few mad waltzes left in us yet.

At 10:30 P.M. one evening, Banning received a phone call from the Brooklyn command post directing him to rent cars for a motorcade on the upcoming weekend. It was a tactical insanity I opposed from the outset. Motorcades are not within the province of municipal politicians. They are the sacred routes taken only by presidents, gods of the world of sport, and explorers of the unknown. We were exempt from the first two categories, and since the soul is not yet a charted celestial body, we couldn't even qualify for the latter.

Besides, a motorcade smacked of panic. I knew well it was a crazy attempt to overcome our "recognition gap" with the voters, the supposed logic being that we would drive through every borough's main thoroughfare and the names of Mailer and Breslin, like salt and pepper, would be sprinkled about every dinner table that evening. In addition to being incredibly difficult to route (even if one has a superstar on the seat), such a project takes a month of expert advance work. Moreover, I felt Mailer was forgetting his mentor: we were losing our grace under pressure.

But such protestations were overruled, and like Mr. Toad we had a weekend of motormania. The candidates sat in a white convertible with red seats, preceded by a sound car announcing their coming. Mailer (ever the strategist) had radio command over the speed of the motorcade, so that the announcement of the candidates' names would set in with the pedestrians before their car came into view. At best, the befuddled weekend strollers waved at the noisy procession as one cheerfully waves at a motorcade of wedding celebrants.

The whole episode only added to the ever growing graffiti on headquarters' walls, where, one noticed, the scribbled art had become meaner these days. Such legends as "Norman Mailer Pissed Here" appeared over the bathroom, along with a quote from the Reverend Billy Graham that had been printed in the *Times* and now was ascribed to Mailer: "I'd rather be clean and dumb than dirty and smart." And after this weekend, someone scrawled: "There will be 5,000 more cops if Mailer is Mayor—for Motorcades."

Our last fling was strictly big league. It involved a fifteen-minute "live" television show and New York Jets' quarterback "Broadway Joe" Namath. The dazzling play unfolded like this: Joe Namath owned a bar on the East Side called Bachelors III, which football commissioner Pete Rozelle ordered him to sell because it was frequented by members of the Mafia. In the commissioner's mind, the mob meant money, money means gambling, gambling could lead to fixing and the death of "The Game," which, most important, meant the death of millions in television money. Namath pleaded innocent to any wrongdoing, and Rozelle concurred that Broadway Joe was as pure in heart as Main Street. But the fact remained that gamblers did frequent the place (as they do every "sports" saloon in the city), and it was a bad image for The Game, *i.e.*, The Money. So, since Rozelle and the National Football League had no immediate plans for a franchise in Sicily, they remained on the side of clean money and ordered Namath to sell. Namath called a press conference, cried (a possible Procaccino man?), refused to sell, and quit football. Enter Breslin.

Jimmy had written a glowing magazine article about Namath earlier in the year. He found the young athlete to have Ruthian significance in the sports world and was even impressed with Namath's "nearly remembering" the names of *all* the broads with whom he had slept. This, I suspected, was Ruthian recall. So, if one is allowed to mix his sports metaphors, Jimmy wanted to go to bat for the quarterback. Enter Mailer.

In the past, Mailer had had no such love affair with Namath. In fact, he argued with Jimmy earlier in the campaign about his magazine article, commenting: "Namath just stands there [in the pocket] stiff-legged and throws the ball." Thus, he was dull. Mailer was a fan of New York Giants' quarterback Fran Tarkenton—"the Scrambler." It was a predictable choice. Tarkenton is a small man with great daring, who scrambles around the backfield, eluding huge linemen until he can complete his play. Such maneuvers had to impress Mailer, whose mind at its most brilliant is the epitome of the double reverse. But now, late in the season, Norman switched sides and agreed with Breslin that the Namath Affair (no double entendre intended) should become our campaign issue.

"The-e-e-e fuckin' hottest issue in the fuckin' city," as Breslin was to proclaim. I thought the candidates had the right issue but the wrong ball park. An election might be carried by Namath in his hometown of Beaver Falls, Pennsylvania, but this was the

Big Apple and another league. And if Mailer was agonizing about the ills of the twentieth century, he should have realized that one of them is forgetting the names of the ladies between whose legs we lay.

But I also suspected the candidates' fascination with the Mafia had something to do with our embroilment. Jimmy had a tendency to make Runyonesque figures out of the mob, and Norman was charmed by "the Maf," as he called it, as it represented clandestine power. One could see him in a backroom arm-wrestling the mob's No. 1 for the soul of the city.

When I presented my arguments for noninvolvement: a fringe issue, we knew nothing of the investigation leading to the allegations, and finally, in his own words, Norman found Namath "dull," Mailer did a bit of mental scrambling that would have done Tarkenton proud. "Yes," he said, "but he beat the Baltimore Colts in the Super Bowl when he was a seventeen-point underdog. And we're the underdogs in the city. That's why we have to go out for him." As usual, I was left panting like a dolt of a lineman, while America's premier scrambler ran for daylight.

Cut to live TV show. The impossible dream had come true but, sadly, too late. Breslin had the bug—he wanted to win. The transformation simply came about because he couldn't bear the thought of one James Breslin losing to a collection of office clerks. He wrote a political ad in the form of his old *Herald Tribune* column and paid to have it printed in the *Post* and the *News*. He wrote a check for $1,700 to cover his half of the television show, an epic which was entitled "Mailer-Breslin Live!"

Never in the annals of "the industry," as the insiders call it, has a television program been put together this way. The only props to be used were blowups of photographs taken by campaign photographer Dick Frank. Breslin asked Mailer what they would do for fifteen minutes, and without the trace of a smile

Mailer answered: "You'll talk for the first seven minutes, and I'll talk for the other eight." And, by God, he meant it! No script. No rehearsal. No notes. And no tape. Just walk in, sit down, and wing it.

It was then I realized the darkest irony of the campaign. The things I cherished in Mailer as a writer—his daring, his unpredictability, his gambling, and his bluffing—were the very things that made me want to strangle him as a politician. It was a revelation that returned my sanity.

Steinem called to tell me that CBS had said they would have a lawyer in the sound booth, and at the first hint of a "fuck" coming from Mailer's mouth he was going to pull a switch that would produce total blackness on the home screen. I had a terrible vision of Norman playing the Southern politician, trying to get folksy, and saying: "Ah, fudge," and as the "fu" sound emerged, our losing $3,400 of air time.

When I arrived at the studio the night of the show, Breslin was sitting in a corner sipping coffee and puffing a cigar, scribbling thoughts on a pad, and talking like hell to himself. Adam Walinsky was at his side, acting as a coach. Mailer was amazingly fresh and buoyant, obviously keyed up for the evening. The TV people were a wreck. Pampered by years of handling safe taped shows, they weren't equal to a live adventure; and the erratic nature of their "stars" didn't help to soothe their nerves. They kept asking Mailer what he was going to do, and Mailer succinctly told them—talk. Cigarettes were being puffed at a rate that would collapse a whale's lungs.

The simple set consisted of two chairs separated by a small table and Frank's blowups. A live audience of about fifty people (there by Mailer's invitation) from Women Strike for Peace and white, Black, and Puerto Rican representatives from community centers around the city sat in folding chairs in front of the stage. Beverly and some of our staff filled the remaining chairs. It was not a "standard" political audience, since some of the dress and hairdos were ethnic (Afros), but neither was it exotic.

Mailer asked if it would be all right if he rose from his chair to speak, and the technicians advised against it. He didn't seem pleased, and with ten minutes to go to air time he ducked out for some liquid inspiration. The cigarette smoke now became so dense the studio could be described as "ceiling zero."

I went into the control booth to watch on the monitors, and the scene in the booth was reminiscent of the television scenes in the Beatles' film *A Hard Day's Night*. Sensitive young men scurried about in sweaters, agonizing: "What in the name of Jesus H. Christ are they going to do?" One prepared for much swooning. Walinsky came into the sound booth to ask me if I was going to "let the camera pan *that* audience as Mailer had instructed?" I informed him that Mailer's wife and invited guests were in *that* audience, and I, indeed, was going to allow the camera to pan it. He called the director aside and told him he didn't think an audience pan would be helpful to the candidates. The rattled director agreed, and liberal "taste" once again replaced courage.

It began. Some small talk about the blowups—"Yeah, I remember that day," etc., and on into Jimmy's seven minutes. Breslin addressed himself to "fear." He said the opposition were trying to frighten the voters, even to the extent of not going out in the streets to vote. (Wagner had done a commercial stating: "If you're going out to vote, don't go alone.") Breslin's presentation was both moving and unnerving. His honesty always was effective when he talked about fear and the Blacks and whites; but sometimes he was so damned adamant about his point, he seemed to be saying: "If you're afraid, I'll kill you, you punks." At the end of his talk, he planned to say to the voters: "So tomorrow let's you and I go out for a walk," but he forgot his line. The camera zoomed in for a close-up, and there was Breslin mouthing nothing. The control booth went into hysteria. "Jesus, pan to Mailer." "What the hell is he moving his mouth for?" "Switch the goddamn camera."

And switch they did. Right from the frying pan to the fire. Mailer reached over and slapped Breslin's hand, the way athletes do, and bounded from his chair, nearly hitting the mike boom with his head. The booth sounded like a poultry slaughterhouse. Shrieks emitted from every chair: "Jesus, he's up," delivered with the incredulity one might have mustered at the Resurrection. "Get that fuckin' boom away from his head." "Switch cameras." (For a moment, the camera moved so abruptly we were rendered a shot of the air above the candidate's heads.) "Lunatic"; "Son of a bitch," they wailed. One thought he could see the alpaca hair on their sweaters wilting.

Mailer made them earn their money. He roamed about the set, puncturing the air with his left hand, necessitating multiple camera switches. But the crowning moment was yet to come. Mailer told his audience that he and Breslin had received the only political endorsement that mattered that day—Joe Namath. It was significant, he said, because "Joe is as nutty as we are."

Jimmy, still on camera in the background, buried his head in his hands, rocking to and fro as if he were sitting shiva. The director screamed: "*What* is he doing? Somebody, somebody, tell me what he is doing."

It finally was over, and I emerged from the sound booth as one leaves an electrode treatment. Beverly defiantly strode up to me and said: "One thing you can say, he wasn't plastic." Neither was Disraeli, I might have added, but he was a politician.

During the closing days of the campaign, the predictable began to happen. Our constituency fell toward the middle, or the left middle—Badillo, in this case. It followed the traditional pattern of American politics. No matter how attractive a border campaign, either left or right, the voters in the closing moments settle for a safer (or saner) vision of their radicalism, hoping for a winner.

But the polls showed something else. Wagner was not being projected the easy winner everyone expected. Various surveys showed a large undecided vote, ranging in some instances from 19 to 24 percent. And if the election was to be decided in the shadows, Procaccino was the rider of the dark horse.

The predictable also happened at headquarters, a turn I was waiting for. We came to life. Election day has a sexuality of its own. It is not necessarily good—neither are bad broads, but they do the trick. The very activity demands life and participation. There are extra phones to be installed, voters to be pulled out, and polling places to be canvassed. It was in this area the volunteers were tremendous. Led by Peister, the Weinsteins, Gil Levine, and Richie Fishman, they shook the staff out of its lobotomized state. Moreover, like the shady ladies mentioned, one began to feel that if there was that much movement, could love be far behind? In short, we thought we might win.

And much to my amazement when I checked out the results of our last two weeks of work, I found we had been efficient. All the election districts that had been assigned to be canvassed were completed. Fishman and his workers had canvassed over 10,000 voters by phone; and more than 1,000,000 pieces of our literature had been circulated throughout the city. So our last two weeks had been a death of the spirit, not of the body. A pleasing revelation to the politician in me, but not to the romantic.

We had taken a suite in the Plaza Hotel to watch the returns. When I arrived with members of the staff, predictably the hangers-on already were there. Maas in rolled-up shirt sleeves, puffing a big cigar and manning two television sets, seemed to be orchestrating the evening Hyannisport style.

Breslin was sincerely worried about how Norman would accept defeat; and I told him we had talked, and he seemed realistic about his chances. It was the closest the two men had ever been during the campaign. Breslin remained at Mailer's side most of the evening in front of the TV set, his arm protectively around the smaller man's shoulder. It was an odd scene—Mailer would survive, because he had gambled; Breslin, because he had hedged his bet.

Only the fool writes drama where there is none. We were through early—dismally through. It was ironic that the technocrats' offspring, the computer, should render Mailer's moment lifeless. The networks' machines projected us with 5 percent of the vote early, and on into the night we were a dull constant.

Mailer was a gracious loser. Once or twice he carped to me about a staff member ("Banning was a Lindsay man all along") or a botched tactic, but his heart really wasn't in it. Breslin, an actor of enormous talent (he could shine even on a dark stage), promised a parade down Fifth Avenue for his constituency.

In the end, each man beat one candidate—Mailer's 41,136 votes to Scheuer's 38,631; and Breslin's 75,480 to Rangel's 71,139. It was the final picture that we weren't expecting. Both parties' right-wing candidates had won. Marchi won by roughly 6,000 votes over Lindsay, and Procaccino defeated Wagner by roughly 31,000 votes and Badillo by 37,000. Mailer's 41,000 could have put either man over the top.

The close City Council presidency was won two days later by Francis X. Smith in a recount. Jimmy had the distinction of beating the only Black man in the race. One began to hear the liberals howl—like the Hounds of the Baskervilles out on the municipal moors.

Banning was the only member of the staff to remain at headquarters throughout the evening. In a phone conversation I asked him to come to the Plaza, but he refused, saying that someone had to manage headquarters, which was bedlam. His reasoning was sound to a point—about 300 bodies over the Fire Department safety limit had managed to crash their way onto the floor to create a dangerous situation—but I also suspected that abused loyalty had to follow its destined course to onanistic martyrdom.

Around eleven o'clock, the candidates arrived at headquarters to concede. Norman, never one to surrender his vision, told the gathering: "If I'm right about this city being on the edge of doom, then heaven help this city, because there's not much to look forward to with the men they elected today." Breslin, forever Irish, knew that wakes were not all wailing. "I am mortified," he said, "to have taken part in a process that required the bars to be closed." And Banning, in a taped interview for an upcoming special on the election, called Mailer "a pompous ass."

So in the end, as in the beginning, democracy prevailed. Jimmy got off another good line, Norman got his hank of hair and what went with it, and Banning got a pound of flesh from a Pulitzer Prize winner on his beloved media.

For me, it was a slower death. Breslin went into hiding, Mailer went to Provincetown to write his moon-shot book, and I went to a saloon, an interlude interrupted by the dismantling of the operation. Bills to be paid, equipment to be returned, and good-byes to be made. To be defeated in battle is one thing, but to linger at the scene of that defeat is quite another. To watch the very life pulled out of our enterprise—the phones, the tables and chairs, the typewriters and calculators, and, most of all, the people—was not a chore for which I was emotionally suited.

The death of anything is tender only in the abstract. In reality, one is left to wipe up the excretions of the corpse. But life has a circular fairness to it. Mailer and Breslin paid their dues by being mortified at the polls. I, a lesser light in the drama, was left with the gravedigger's detail.

7
A Small Benediction
(Epilogue)

O N November 10, John V. Lindsay, running on the Liberal Party and Independent lines, defeated John Marchi (Republican-Conservative) and Mario Procaccino (Democrat) for mayor by receiving 42 percent of the vote. Thus, the city of New York once more upheld its liberal tradition. Or did it?

Marchi and Procaccino, both tough "law and order" candidates, received 58 percent of the vote between them (Procaccino —35 percent, Marchi—23 percent), enabling Lindsay to win in a three-way race. The profound perversity to be plumbed by his liberal critics is: Did Mailer save the city for liberalism?

Suppose Mailer had withdrawn (or had not entered) and 37,000 of his 41,000 votes had gone to Badillo (a projection that the liberal press in retrospect carved in granite); and the cards came up Badillo vs. Marchi with Lindsay running on the Liberal line, a commitment he had to make to Liberal Party boss Alex Rose before receiving that party's nomination. So then the city would have had a situation in which the liberal vote would have been splintered and the conservative vote solidified behind one man.

But I don't at all believe that Mailer's vote was transferable to Badillo, so if the liberals would have the grace to end their paranoia, I will have the modesty not to claim that I was the architect of a master plan to save the city for "humanism."

But what about us? Like Willy Loman's nagging wife who wanted to know what happened in Boston, the question that has dogged our days since the primary has been: What did it all mean? To us it meant simply that a group of men who loved their city thought they had a set of ideas that might save that city and gave those ideas light. It can be argued that as writers we set out on an arrogant enterprise. Our lives, financially or otherwise, were there to be picked up if we lost.

It can be said that we should have left the field open for the first Puerto Rican candidate for mayor. In fact, that was an argument fostered by many in liberal circles: "Herman would be our first Puerto Rican mayor," an argument that found no sympathy with me. This sentiment, I suppose, could be construed as "a white man's," and if this is the arena in which our critics wish to fight, then all I can say is that I simply exercised my whiteness.

Our run has to stand on the ideas we put forth, and I think it stands firm. If we are to be judged and disdained for the stupidity, the pettiness, the meanness, the laughing, and the drinking recounted in this book, the reader should keep two thoughts in his head: first, I believe I have told more than other chroniclers of campaigns; second, if the above traits are abhorrent, then most of mankind is in that lamentable state.

Theodore White, author of *The Making of the President* series, looked *only* at the product of our work and had this to say: "One of the most serious campaigns run in the United States in the last five years was Norman Mailer's. I didn't vote for him, but his campaign was considered and thoughtful, the beginning of an attempt to apply ideas to a political situation. The job of intellectuals is to come up with ideas, and all we've been producing is footnotes."

And, obviously, our ideas had wings. After the primary, a Lindsay aide called and requested our position papers, and the office of the mayor of Milwaukee made the same request. The good burghers of that city, according to the mayor's aide, are going to have a chance to vote for their statehood in the next election. So, in some corners anyway, we did what we intended—dramatized the death of the cities.

Where did we go wrong? Basically, by saying what we thought. Pap is much more the diet of the electorate, and that isn't meant to sound like a whine. What really led us astray was a faulty premise. We forgot an old lesson: Most men take their politics very lightly and their politicians very seriously. In short, was Walinsky darkly brilliant when he said, "Look like the other guys"? I'm sure my hairy tale would pale next to the boobery that took place in the Procaccino camp or the inside bloodletting and manipulation conducted by that Macbeth of the Pedernales, LBJ.

Next, there was our spiritual romanticism. We ran on the premise that men really want to control their own government, a proposition that entails a huge expenditure of individual involvement and time. We are a people who like to play, not to do penance. Our campaign took the claim of the conservatives —that big government is evil—to heart, only to find what they were saying was that the "wrong kind" of big government is evil. Sadly, our beloved working class was only seeking to shift the weapon of power from the left hip to the right.

And last but very important, I failed. I was the wrong man for the job. We should have hired a professional to run the campaign for two reasons: he would have been capable of the task; and a professional could have commanded much more control of the candidates than a young writer beneath their literary stature. So when the song goes sour, it isn't always proper to shoot the piano player, but in this instance take dead aim on the guy with the baton. Yet this is a lament with an "if" tagged on. Because "if" I had to do it all over again, all I can say is: "Once a philosopher—twice a pervert."

The very reason we were able to say what we pleased and on our good days be impudent to political mores was because we were amateurs. This is the blessing of a "bastard" or an "irresponsible" campaign. Our ideas will never see light in the pure form we delivered them, but now one hears talk in the city of "home rule" and "neighborhood city halls." As Picasso once said about new forms: "We do it first. Then someone comes along and pretties it up, and the public buys it."

In the end it was a campaign without heroes save the young volunteers. A graceful generation that had to work for men wrapped up in their individual egos, a sin their flesh is not heir to. But they were equally hard for us to fathom—a group that is buoyed by the collective purity of their age, an aspect as frightening to us as our individual posturing was to them. And our defeat was easier for them, because they could curse time. Mailer and Breslin could curse only themselves.

Even though it was a party from which we didn't get to take home the girl, I'm glad I attended. For in a city where men of ideas usually are satisfied to swap love notes with their contemporaries in precious little quarterlies, like convicts in a cellblock, Mailer and Breslin went out and had "a dubious fuck with that mean woman," the city of New York.

Since we ran to win and Breslin scored highest, it is only fitting that our gutter genius have the last say. What follows is his prophecy which appeared in the New York *Times:* "Ten years from now there'll be a big inauguration for the State of New York City, and they'll send me and Norman the wrong colored tickets, and we'll be stumbling around trying to find our seats way up at the top of the stadium, and people will look at us and say, 'They're drunk.'"

Amen.